SAN LEANDRO High

Dian Fossey

These and other titles are included in The Importance
Of biography series:

"I wish to express my deepest gratitude to the gorillas of the mountains for having permitted me to come to know them as the uniquely noble individuals that they are."

Dian Fossey, *Gorillas in the Mist*

THE IMPORTANCE OF

Dian Fossey

by
Jack Roberts

Lucent Books, P.O. Box 289011, San Diego, CA 92198-9011

Library of Congress Cataloging-in-Publication Data

Roberts, Jack L.
    Dian Fossey / by Jack Roberts.
        p. cm.—(The Importance of)
    Includes bibliographical references (p.   ) and index.
    ISBN 1-56006-068-9 (alk. paper)
    1. Fossey, Dian—Juvenile literature.   2. Gorilla—Rwanda—
Juvenile literature.   3. Primatologists—United States—Biography
—Juvenile literature. [1. Fossey, Dian. 2. Zoologists. 3. Gorilla.
4. Women—Biography.]   I.Title. II. Series.
QL31.F65R63   1995
599.88'46'092—dc20   94-6841
[B]   CIP
                                                                  AC

Contents

Foreword

THE IMPORTANCE OF biography series deals with individuals who have made a unique contribution to history. The editors of the series have deliberately chosen to cast a wide net and include people from all fields of endeavor. Individuals from politics, music, art, literature, philosophy, science, sports, and religion are all represented. In addition, the editors did not restrict the series to individuals whose accomplishments have helped change the course of history. Of necessity, this criterion would have eliminated many whose contribution was great, though limited. Charles Darwin, for example, was responsible for radically altering the scientific view of the natural history of the world. His achievements continue to impact the study of science today. Others, such as Chief Joseph of the Nez Percé, played a pivotal role in the history of their own people. While Joseph's influence does not extend much beyond the Nez Percé, his nonviolent resistance to white expansion and his continuing role in protecting his tribe and his homeland remain an inspiration to all.

These biographies are more than factual chronicles. Each volume attempts to emphasize an individual's contributions both in his or her own time and for posterity. For example, the voyages of Christopher Columbus opened the way to European colonization of the New World. Unquestionably, his encounter with the New World brought monumental changes to both Europe and the Americas in his day. Today, however, the broader impact of Columbus's voyages is being critically scrutinized. *Christopher Columbus,* as well as every biography in The Importance Of series, includes and evaluates the most recent scholarship available on each subject.

Each author includes a wide variety of primary and secondary source quotations to document and substantiate his or her work. All quotes are footnoted to show readers exactly how and where biographers derive their information, as well as to provide stepping stones to further research. These quotations enliven the text by giving readers eyewitness views of the life and times of each individual covered in The Importance Of series.

Finally, each volume is enhanced by photographs, bibliographies, chronologies, and comprehensive indexes. For both the casual reader and the student engaged in research, The Importance Of biographies will be a fascinating adventure into the lives of people who have helped shape humanity's past and present, and who will continue to shape its future.

Important Dates in the Life of Dian Fossey

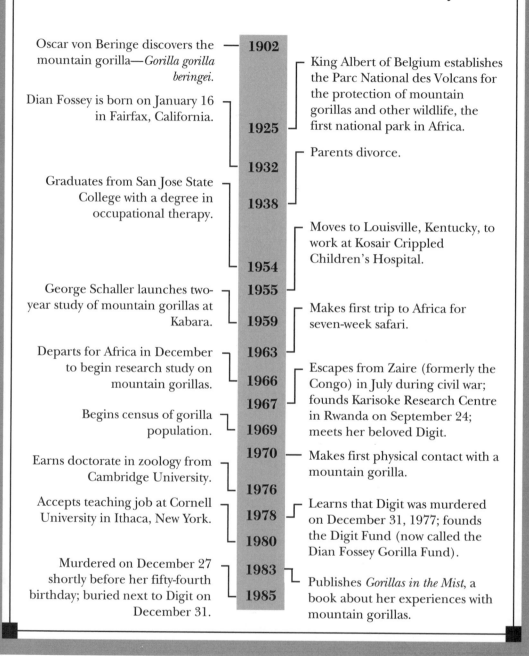

Oscar von Beringe discovers the mountain gorilla—*Gorilla gorilla beringei.*

1902

King Albert of Belgium establishes the Parc National des Volcans for the protection of mountain gorillas and other wildlife, the first national park in Africa.

Dian Fossey is born on January 16 in Fairfax, California.

1925

1932 Parents divorce.

Graduates from San Jose State College with a degree in occupational therapy.

1938

Moves to Louisville, Kentucky, to work at Kosair Crippled Children's Hospital.

1954

George Schaller launches two-year study of mountain gorillas at Kabara.

1955

1959 Makes first trip to Africa for seven-week safari.

Departs for Africa in December to begin research study on mountain gorillas.

1963

1966

1967 Escapes from Zaire (formerly the Congo) in July during civil war; founds Karisoke Research Centre in Rwanda on September 24; meets her beloved Digit.

Begins census of gorilla population.

1969

1970 Makes first physical contact with a mountain gorilla.

Earns doctorate in zoology from Cambridge University.

1976

Accepts teaching job at Cornell University in Ithaca, New York.

1978

1980 Learns that Digit was murdered on December 31, 1977; founds the Digit Fund (now called the Dian Fossey Gorilla Fund).

Murdered on December 27 shortly before her fifty-fourth birthday; buried next to Digit on December 31.

1983

1985 Publishes *Gorillas in the Mist,* a book about her experiences with mountain gorillas.

A Life Devoted to the Gentle Giants

"Dian kufa! Dian kufa!" yelled Kanyaragana, a camp worker at Karisoke Research Centre in the tiny African country of Rwanda. "Dian kufa! Dian kufa!" he yelled as he ran across the lush green meadow toward Wayne McGuire's cabin.

It was 5:45 A.M. on Thursday, December 27, 1985. McGuire, an American graduate student who had arrived at Karisoke only five months earlier, knew only a few words in Swahili. But he instantly understood those chilling words. "Dian kufa." *Dian is dead.*

A few minutes later McGuire and the camp staff rushed into Dian Fossey's tiny, two-room cabin. There, lying on the floor beside her bed, was the most famous primatologist in the world with "a brutal gash [running] diagonally across her forehead, over the top of her nose, and down her cheek."[1]

McGuire went numb. How, he must have wondered, could this have happened? Who could have murdered the woman who had become known throughout the world as the savior of the moun-

Dian Fossey in 1970, four years after she left for Africa to study the mountain gorillas.

tain gorilla? For McGuire the answers to those questions would eventually have devastating personal consequences.

An Unlikely Beginning

Twenty years earlier, when Dian Fossey first went to Africa to begin a long-term study of the nearly extinct mountain gorillas, no one could possibly have imagined that she would one day be recognized as one of the foremost primatologists in the world. For one thing, she lacked a background in zoology, the science that deals with the animal kingdom. For another, she simply didn't have the necessary research skills.

What's more, Fossey was thirty-four years old when she first began her study in Africa, and she was not in good health. She had had asthma as a child and suffered frequently from pneumonia as an adult. To make matters worse, she suffered from acrophobia, a tremendous fear of heights. How could she possibly think about crawling around the rugged terrain of a mountain ten thousand feet high?

Finally, Fossey knew virtually nothing about living in a rain forest on a mountain in Africa. She didn't know the language, nor did she know anything about the customs of the local people—the Bahutu, the Watusi, and the Batwa.

By contrast, her predecessor in the study of mountain gorillas, Dr. George B. Schaller, was an ideal candidate for such a project. Dr. Schaller had degrees in both zoology and anthropology and he was a highly trained researcher and scientist. He was also only twenty-six years old when he went to Africa to study the gorillas in 1959, and he was in excellent health.

Yet, what Fossey lacked in education, training, and physical strength, she made up for in persistence, courage, and hard work. But mostly she possessed sheer determination. Once Fossey made up her mind to do something—even something as crazy as living alone on a mountain in Africa—no one could change her mind. "It was this persistence, this determination to stay in the field despite all difficulties, discomforts, and dangers that led, I believe, to her most significant contribution to science," says Jane Goodall, another primatologist whose work with chimpanzees in Tanzania is as famous as Fossey's work with mountain gorillas.[2]

The Discovery of Mountain Gorillas

For eighteen years Fossey lived and worked on the Virunga Mountains, a chain of eight volcanic mountains that shares the boundaries of three countries in east-central Africa: Rwanda, Zaire (formerly the Congo), and Uganda. It was here on the Virunga Mountains that the mountain gorilla was first discovered in 1902. A German officer named Oscar von Beringe was climbing Mount Sabinyo in Rwanda when he came upon "large black apes." Although these gorillas were similar to gorillas found in West Africa, they had certain characteristics that made them distinctly different. Consequently, this subspecies of gorilla was given the scientific name *Gorilla gorilla beringei*, in honor of its discoverer.

After the discovery of these mountain gorillas, many American and European hunters and adventurers traveled to the Virungas to shoot and kill the great apes and bring their bodies back to museums for display. One of the American hunters was a man named Carl Akeley, who was also a taxidermist. During a trip to the Virungas in 1921 Akeley shot five gorillas for the American Museum of Natural History in New York City.

Yet, through his observation of the mountain gorilla, Akeley soon realized that it was "normally a perfectly amiable

The Virunga Mountains where Fossey would spend eighteen years studying the mountain gorilla. The mountains were virtually inaccessible to humans.

and decent creature."[3] He also realized that the gorillas were in danger of becoming extinct, so he decided to try to do something to protect them.

At that time Rwanda and the Congo were territories of Belgium. So, Akeley went to the king of Belgium, Albert, and convinced him to create a sanctuary or preserve for the mountain gorillas—a place where the gorillas and other wildlife would be protected from hunters. This preserve, which was established in 1925, was named Albert National Park in his honor. It was the first national park in all of Africa.

Carl Akeley originally hunted mountain gorillas, killing them for museums. He later helped establish the first national park to protect the vulnerable animals.

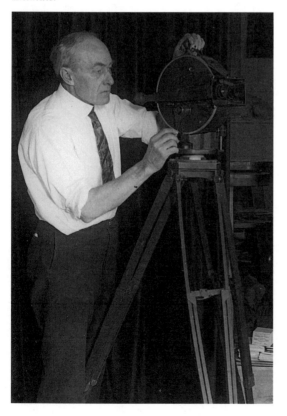

In the 1960s Rwanda and the Congo gained their independence. At that time Albert National Park became known as the Parc National des Virungas on the Zaire side, and the Parc National des Volcans on the Rwanda side. (A small portion of the preserve in Uganda had already become known as the Kigezi Gorilla Sanctuary in 1930.)

In 1926 Akeley returned to Africa, this time to study, rather than kill, the gorillas. He planned to set up his camp on a small meadow named Kabara, located in a flat area, or saddle, between Mount Mikeno and Mount Karisimbi, two of the eight Virunga Mountains. Unfortunately, before he could begin his research, he caught pneumonia and died. His wife, who was with him on the trip, had him buried at Kabara Meadow.

The First Study of Mountain Gorillas

Thirty-three years later, in 1959, an American scientist named George Schaller and his wife Kay went to Mount Mikeno and Kabara Meadow along with John Emlen, a professor of zoology at the University of Wisconsin, to begin the research that Akeley never had a chance to conduct. For the next two years Schaller and his team observed and studied the mountain gorillas of the Virungas. What he discovered was quite different from the commonly held belief about these animals. They were not belligerent, ferocious beasts, as they had so often been portrayed. Instead, Schaller's study showed that for the most part the mountain gorillas were really only gentle giants, who would charge toward

someone only if they sensed danger to their family.

During his study, Schaller recognized the mountain gorillas as individuals "each with foibles, sensitivities, problems, family ties, traditions, and past experience."[4] His study of the mountain gorillas provided the most definitive information available about these animals until Fossey arrived in Africa to study them in 1966.

An Enigmatic Paradox

When Dian Fossey first arrived in Africa, only 242 mountain gorillas were left in all of the Virungas, according to the best estimates. She had been selected to head up a long-term study of the mountain gorillas by Dr. Louis S.B. Leakey, a renowned anthropologist and the most eminent scientist in the world in the study of primates.

Fossey wanted her research work to pick up where Schaller's left off. Specifi-

American scientist George Schaller (above) was one of the first to study the mountain gorillas (right). He found them to be sensitive and social.

cally, she wanted to "form more intimate contacts with gorilla groups and individuals, to observe from close up their behavior, their interactions, and to do this in such a way that my [her] presence did not affect that behavior."[5]

During the first six years of her work in Africa, she accomplished many of her research objectives. But, over time, she became less interested in her field studies, and more interested in saving the gorillas. She became their self-appointed protector, waging war against anyone or anything that she saw as a threat to her mountain gorillas. This included hunters, or poachers, who illegally hunted duiker, or antelope, in the preserve, but who also often caught mountain gorillas in their snares. It included herdsmen with their hundreds of head of cattle that grazed on the mountainside, trampling the vegetation. It included tourists or "noisy busybodies," as she liked to call them. And, in the end, it even included Rwandan government officials.

In many ways Fossey was a paradox. Some saw her as a soft-spoken, even shy, young woman. Others knew she could be amazingly aggressive—a real street fighter, particularly when it came to her beloved

Fossey went to Africa to establish human contact with the gorillas and study their social groups. Here, she holds an infant gorilla, proof that she accomplished her goal.

A Misinformed Perception

The view that the mountain gorilla was a ferocious man killer with superhuman strength was generally credited to Paul Du Chaillu, who described the gorilla in Explorations and Adventures in Equatorial Africa.

"His eyes began to flash fire as we stood motionless on the defensive . . . while his powerful fangs were shown as he again sent forth a thunderous roar. And now truly he reminded me of nothing but some hellish dream creature—a being of that hideous order, half-man half-beast. . . . He advanced a few steps, then stopped to utter that hideous roar again—advanced again, and finally stopped when at a distance of about six yards from us. And there, just as he began another of his roars, beating his breast in rage, we fired and killed him."

gorillas. Some saw her as a "fearless savior who dedicated her life to the animals she loved; others as a lonely, bitter vigilante."[6] Perhaps she was both.

Clearly, her life and her work were not without controversy. And eventually the protection of the mountain gorilla became an obsession as strong as any a mother or father has to protect her or his child. For in many ways the mountain gorillas were her family. She treated them as if they were her children. And, in return, she believed that they truly did love her.

For nearly twenty years Fossey devoted her life to these gentle giants, almost single-handedly bringing the plight of the mountain gorilla to the attention of the world. "Had it not been for Dian Fossey," said the president of the National Geographic Society at the time of Fossey's death, "there is no doubt in my mind that the mountain gorilla would by now have joined the list of extinct species."[7]

Yet, her obsession with protecting the mountain gorilla at all costs eventually began to get in the way of good sense and rational judgment. By the time she was murdered, Fossey had developed dozens of enemies, not only among the people of Rwanda, but among her American and European students as well. "I think by the end she was doing more harm than good," says a former student.[8]

Today many people question whether Dian Fossey's greatest contribution was as a scientific researcher or as an active conservationist. Perhaps the fact that the mountain gorilla still survives today in its natural habitat is the real testament to the importance of Dian Fossey's fascinating and courageous life.

Chapter

1 A Lonely Beginning

Throughout her life Dian Fossey rarely talked about her parents and her own lonely childhood. But this much is known for sure. She was born in Fairfax, California, on Sunday, January 16, 1932. Her father, George Fossey, was an insurance salesman, who some say was also an alcoholic. Her mother, Hazel, also known as Kitty, was a beautiful woman who worked as a fashion model for San Francisco clothing stores.

In 1938, when Fossey was six years old, her mother and father divorced, and George Fossey disappeared from his young daughter's life completely. Soon after the divorce Kitty married a man named Richard Price, a fairly well-to-do building contractor. A strict disciplinarian,

Fossey was born in Fairfax, near the metropolitan area of San Francisco (pictured). Alienated from her mother and unable to relate to her stepfather, Fossey's childhood was marked by loneliness.

Fossey always had a natural affinity for animals, especially horses. This prompted her to work on a dude ranch in Montana one summer.

Price was not particularly fond of children and never legally adopted Fossey. Consequently, Fossey was often starved for affection and love, which she reportedly never received from either her mother or her stepfather.

Some say Fossey grew up deeply resenting both her mother and her stepfather and would refer to them in later years as "the Prices." Others say she actually hated Price and would "spit on the ground whenever her stepfather's name was mentioned."[9] But Fossey's mother adamantly disagrees. She says her daughter loved her stepfather. And the fact is that Fossey did stay in touch with both her mother and stepfather throughout her life, visiting them whenever she returned to the United States from her adopted homeland in Africa.

As a young girl Fossey developed a great love for animals, particularly horses. She took riding lessons when she was in elementary school and in high school was a member of the riding club. In college she kept her own horse in a stable near the school.

As a child she developed many illnesses, including asthma. As an adult she suffered from many different allergies and tended to get pneumonia frequently.

By the time Fossey was fourteen years old, she was six feet one inch tall and self-conscious about her height. Part of the reason for this uneasiness may have been that her own mother was embarrassed by it. At one point Kitty Price even took her daughter to a doctor to see if he could do anything about it. As one friend said years later, "I think Mrs. Price made Dian feel she was too big, too awkward, that she was no great beauty, and that she wouldn't be received well in good company."[10]

As a result, Dian grew up not having a good self-image. And she was painfully shy around people. Yet, she loved animals. One summer she worked at a dude ranch in Montana. A young man who worked with her there remembers that she was "completely wrapped up in animals—the horses, dogs, a pet coyote, anything that walked or flew."[11]

Fossey graduated from Lowell High School in 1948 and that fall enrolled in a business course at Marin Junior College in Kentfield, California. Two years later she enrolled as a pre-veterinary medical student at the University of California at Davis. She wanted to become a veterinarian, but it soon became apparent that her high school science grades were not good

Two Kinds of Animal Lovers

Some people, as author Alex Shoumatoff writes in his book African Madness, *develop an extraordinary relationship with animals as a result of a very lonely childhood.*

"In general, people who are drawn to nature and become animal lovers fall into two groups, which might be described as the Shakespeareans and the Thoreauvians. The Shakespeareans consider man and his works to be part of nature; while loving animals, they have warm, positive feelings toward people, too. The animal love of the Thoreauvians, however, is inversely proportionate to their compassion for their own kind. Often their problems with people, and their sometimes extraordinary empathy with animals, can be traced to a lonely childhood."

enough for her to qualify for veterinary school. So she transferred to San Jose State College in San Jose, California, where she majored in occupational therapy.

As graduation approached in 1954, Fossey began looking for a job as an occupational therapist. As she searched the help wanted advertisements in newspapers and special magazines, she had only two requirements for her job: one, it had to take her as far away from California and her stepfather as possible, and two, it had to be near horses.

Starting a Career in Kentucky

One day, simply by chance, Fossey saw an advertisement for an occupational therapist at Kosair Crippled Children's Hospital in Louisville, Kentucky. Not only was Louisville the home of the Kentucky Derby, the most important and prestigious thoroughbred horse race in the country, but it was also more than two thousand miles away from California—far enough from her family that it must have seemed perfect to the young woman.

Fossey immediately wrote to the hospital to apply for the job. To her surprise, she got it, and by September 1955 she had the title of Director of the Occupational Therapy Department at Kosair Crippled Children's Hospital. Despite the impressive-sounding title, however, she earned less than $5,300 a year.

At that time a terrible virus called poliomyelitis, or polio, was affecting many people throughout the country, particularly young children. People who were infected with polio often developed paralysis of the legs or atrophy—degeneration—of certain skeletal muscles. Many of the young children at Kosair at that time were victims of polio.

Other children there suffered from emotional problems. Many were withdrawn and wouldn't communicate with anyone. "These children have a variety of physical and emotional disabilities and are lost in this world of ours," Fossey once explained. "All are much younger than their years and are like wild animals penned up with no hope of escape. They need a tremendous amount of care and kindness to make them feel life is worth living."[12]

Fossey had a special talent for working with these children. She never pushed herself on them. Rather, she would quietly visit them in their rooms, sometimes pre-

Polio ravaged the United States during the 1950s, permanently paralyzing many children. After graduating from college, Fossey worked at a hospital caring for victims of the disease.

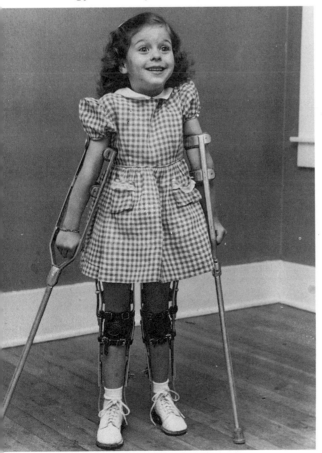

tending to ignore them altogether. Many people thought her behavior was odd. Yet, it seemed to work. Gradually the young children grew to trust her and open up to her. Years later Fossey used this same approach in getting gorillas used to her presence and in gaining their trust.

Her Life in Louisville

As soon as Fossey arrived in Louisville, she rented a small cottage on a large, old estate outside of town. At first the owner of the estate did not want to rent the house to her. He felt the property was too far from town and too isolated for a young girl to live there by herself. But Fossey insisted that being alone was exactly what she wanted, and in the end, the landlord agreed. Fossey moved in and remained in the small cottage for the next ten years.

In 1959 Fossey received a letter from her father, George, who begged her to write to him. They began an occasional correspondence that lasted until his death in 1968. During this time, she had strongly ambivalent feelings about him. As one of Fossey's former boyfriends explained, "On the one hand, he could do no wrong. He was a wonderful man, misunderstood— the usual nonsense. On the other, when she saw the reality of how she'd been treated by him, she didn't like it at all."[13]

Nevertheless, years later when Fossey was a famous primatologist, she gave her father credit for her interest in wildlife. "I wonder what he would think of the Virungas," she once wrote in her diary. "He always did love the wilderness, but never had a chance to enjoy it very much. Perhaps I'm here because of that."[14]

Few people got to know Fossey very well during the years she lived in Louisville. But those who did say that she always gave the impression that she liked animals better than people. This reputation stayed with her the rest of her life, even though at least one friend of Fossey's during her later years maintains that the reputation was unfair and untrue.

Yet, those people who did get to know Fossey during her years in Louisville seemed to enjoy her company. One friend says that she was "a neat person to be with —generous to a fault, extraordinarily disciplined, with a delightful, self-deprecating sense of humor, tall, slim, perfectly gorgeous."[15]

Fossey's best friend at that time was a young woman named Mary White Henry, who came from a prominent family in Louisville. Fossey fell in love with the en-

tire Henry family, possibly because it was so unlike her own. She developed a particular attachment to Gaynee Henry, Mary White's mother, who became a surrogate mother to Fossey.

Mary White introduced Fossey to many of the most eligible bachelors in Louisville. But Fossey was interested in a young man named Pookie Forrester, the son of a wealthy family from Africa.

Franz Joseph Forrester, Pookie's father, was an Austrian count who had escaped from the Nazis during World War II and moved his family to Rhodesia (now called Zimbabwe), located in southern Africa. There, they started a successful tobacco farm.

The Forresters had been friends with the Henry family for many years. One year, when Pookie was visiting the United States, he stopped in to visit the Henry

Fossey lived in Louisville, Kentucky, immediately after graduating from college. She rented a small cottage on the outskirts of town, preferring the isolation to the city.

Her Home in Louisville

In Woman in the Mists, *Farley Mowat provides insight to Fossey's life at her home in Louisville. This quotation is from the diary she kept during that time.*

"Never have I seen any place as beautiful as this is now in autumn. . . . The creeks are full of the golden, red, green, and brown leaves from the forests. The pastures are still vivid green and are framed by trees that you would swear were on fire. When I wake up in the morning, I just run to the windows all over the house and am blinded by the beauty. Quite often I'll see a raccoon or possum scurrying by, or else the ninety head of Angus cattle will be taking their morning meal off my backyard. When I come home from work, I have to take about twenty minutes to feed the multitude of barn cats and the big white shepherd dog from over the hill who stops by for a handout, along with our own farm dogs, Mitzi, Shep, and Brownie, who have adopted me as one of their own."

family. There, he met Fossey, whom he immediately liked. Fossey also liked this handsome young man, even though he was seven years younger than she. "He's a dream," she confided to her friend Mary White Henry.[16]

After Pookie returned to Africa, he wrote to Fossey constantly. He even talked about marriage. For a while, people thought that the two might become serious. At one point, he even offered to pay her way to Africa for a visit. But something held her back. Even though she wanted to go to Africa very badly, she refused his invitation.

In 1960 Mary White Henry went on a trip to Africa. After Mary returned, Fossey listened to her friend's exciting tales of her wonderful adventure and looked at the glorious pictures of her African safari with a great deal of envy and excitement.

She decided then and there that she too would make a trip to Africa before the end of 1963. There was just one problem. She didn't have enough money for such a trip. And on her meager salary at Kosair, she had very little hope of saving enough on her own.

Africa "Madness"

Reluctantly, she decided to ask her parents for a loan. But they refused, saying that the trip was both foolish and dangerous. Even her favorite aunt and uncle thought the idea of going off to Africa was, as they put it, "madness."

But Fossey was determined to get there one way or another. Finally, she managed to get a loan from a bank at an outrageously high interest rate. As Fossey later recalled, "I committed myself to a three-year bank debt in order to finance a seven-week safari."[17]

Years later, in her book *Gorillas in the Mist*, Fossey acknowledges the Henrys for their support of her dream to go to Africa. "Many of us have dreams or ambitions we hope to fulfill someday," she said. "My own, to go to Africa to study the mountain gorillas, might never have succeeded had it not been for the Henry family of Louisville, Kentucky."[18]

So, on September 26, 1963, Dian Fossey departed for Africa. As she put it, "After months spent planning my itinerary, most of which was far off the normal tourist routes, I hired a driver, by mail, from a Nairobi safari company and flew to the land of my dreams."[19]

Chapter

2 Africa: The Land of Her Dreams

"Two of the main goals of my first African trip," Fossey claims in her book *Gorillas in the Mist*, "were to visit the mountain gorillas of Mt. Mikeno in the Congo and to meet Louis and Mary Leakey at Olduvai Gorge in Tanzania."[20] While both goals came true for this adventurous young woman, some people insist today that before Fossey left for Africa, she had never heard of either mountain gorillas or Dr. Leakey.

Author Harold T.P. Hayes, for example, says it was only after she got to Africa that she learned about mountain gorillas from a biologist named Jacques Veschuren. He also says that Fossey's guide in Africa, John Alexander, maintains it was his idea to stop at Olduvai, not Fossey's.

Yet Fossey evidently wanted people to have a certain image of her as a woman who had been devoted to mountain gorillas all of her life. So, when she wrote her book, she conveniently rewrote history, her critics say, to suit herself. It would not be the last time she would do so.

Whatever the truth may be, the fact is that as soon as Fossey arrived in Nairobi, Kenya, in 1963 she went immediately to the Mount Kenya Safari Club where she met her safari guide, Alexander. Together they planned a thousand-mile safari that would take Fossey through East Africa—from Nairobi to Tsavo National Park to

Tanganyika (now Tanzania) and the Serengeti Plain to the Mara River country, then through southwest Kenya back up to Nairobi. She would see the beauty of the African animals up close—everything

Fossey with a Kenyan girl on her first trip to Africa in 1963. Then a tourist, Fossey would return to Africa to study the mountain gorilla.

from elephants to rhinos to the tree-dwelling lions of Lake Manyara National Park. It was, indeed, a trip of a lifetime.

A Visit to Olduvai

During her trip Fossey stopped at Olduvai Gorge in Tanzania (between the conservation area of Ngorongoro Crater and Serengeti). Here she met Dr. Louis S.B. Leakey, the most famous paleoanthropologist in the world at the time, and his wife Mary, who was also a scientist.

In her book Fossey maintains that Louis Leakey spoke with her at length during her visit, not only about her interest in mountain gorillas but about his interest in setting up a long-term field study of the great apes. "How vividly I still can recall Dr. Leakey's sparkling interest in hearing that I was on my way to visit briefly the gorillas at Kabara in the Congolese sector of the Virunga Mountains," she said.[21]

Dr. Louis Leakey and his wife Mary. Fossey credited the famous anthropologist with inspiring her interest in the mountain gorilla.

This recollection may be yet another example of how Fossey has conveniently rewritten history to suit herself. Leakey was quite ill on the day Fossey visited

An Unlikely Candidate

Fossey was a highly unlikely candidate to study the mountain gorillas. One biographer, Harold T.P. Hayes, explains why in his book The Dark Romance of Dian Fossey.

"Fossey was clearly unfit. . . . She was too fragile for the Virungas—and too naïve. . . . She was an American tourist. How could she be expected to cope? Any list of the skills she lacked would just be endless.

She knew nothing of the local languages. . . . She knew nothing of the mountain rain forest, nothing about the wet clinging vegetation, the constant mud; the steep slopes, the hidden ravines; the endless rain and fog, the periodic hailstorms; wet clothes and wet tents that never dried."

Olduvai, and, according to his wife, had very little to do with Fossey. "She was just another tourist," Mary Leakey says.[22]

Oddly enough, in an article Fossey wrote for the *Louisville Courier Journal* after her return from this trip, she herself says that Leakey was sick when she arrived at Olduvai and unable to spend much time with her. According to author Harold Hayes, Fossey "had seen Leakey but he had no time for her. He was suffering from a bout of emphysema. They didn't talk about anything at all."[23]

One thing that everyone agrees on, however, is that while Fossey was visiting Olduvai, she had an accident in which she broke her ankle. She was climbing down into the gorge to see the fossils of a prehistoric giraffe when she slipped and fell. "As the ankle cracked, the sudden pain induced me to vomit unceremoniously all over the treasured fossil," Fossey claims in her book.[24]

Both Mary Leakey and Fossey's guide urged Fossey not to continue with her plans to go to Kabara. It was a difficult five-hour climb up Mount Mikeno to the Kabara Meadow, they told her. She simply would not be able to make it.

But neither of them had any idea just what a determined individual Fossey was. As she later recalled, "Neither of them realized that the accident only strengthened my determination to get to the gorillas I had come to meet in Africa."[25] So, despite the pain, and despite the fact that she could not get her boot on, she continued on her quest to see the gorillas.

The Traveller's Rest

Two weeks after visiting the Leakeys, Fossey and her guide arrived on October 16 at the Traveller's Rest Inn, ideally located at the junction where the Uganda, Rwanda, and Congo borders meet. There, Fossey met Walter Baumgartel, the owner and host of the modest hotel. Since the mid-1950s Baumgartel and his guide Reuben had taken adventure seekers up Mount Mikeno in search of mountain gorillas. As a result, the Traveller's Rest had

Although Fossey was a tourist on her first trip to Africa, she didn't stick to the usual tourist escapades. Instead, she hired a guide to take her into the reaches of the Congo to Kabara Meadow.

gained the reputation as the unofficial gorilla headquarters for Central Africa.

That night Baumgartel told Fossey and her guide fascinating stories about his adventures in Africa and about his observations of mountain gorillas. It is likely that Fossey asked Baumgartel if he thought gorillas were dangerous. That was a question, he said, that all guests at the Traveller's Rest asked. His answer was always the same. "I wouldn't call them perfectly gentle," he would say. Then, he would confess, "As a matter of fact, I was shaken to the core every time I came close to a gorilla."[26]

Before retiring for the night, Baumgartel told Fossey and her guide how to get to the mountain gorillas. First, they should go across the border from Uganda into the Congo and proceed to the park headquarters in Rumangabo, about a two-hour drive from Kisoro. From Rumangabo, they would begin their climb up Mount Mikeno toward the Kabara Meadow.

Kabara Meadow

Fossey could hardly contain her sense of excitement and adventure as she and her guide arrived at the park headquarters the next day. From there, they went to Kibumba, a small village at the foot of the mountain, where they hired a dozen porters to carry their camping gear up the mountain.

For Fossey, the climb up the rugged terrain was excruciating. "It took six and a half hours to get to this camp and I thought I would die," she later said. "My rib cage was bursting, my legs were creaking and in agony, and my ankle felt as though a crocodile had his jaws around it."[27]

Finally, they walked into the clearing of Kabara Meadow—the "place of rest"—the place that Carl Akeley had described as "the most beautiful spot in the world."[28] Little did she know at that time that Kabara Meadow would one day—in the not too distant future—be her home.

There she met Joan and Alan Root, two young but famous wildlife photographers who were camped at the meadow. At first they seemed to resent the intrusion of this young American woman and her guide at Kabara.

The Roots were polite but cool to Fossey and certainly did not volunteer to take her into the forest to see mountain gorillas. Consequently, Fossey and Alexander spent their first day at Kabara simply wandering about the mountainside, but seeing nothing. Eventually, however, Fossey

Wildlife photographers Joan and Alan Root took Fossey into the forest with them on her first trip to Africa. She first came face-to-face with the mountain gorilla on this journey.

won the Roots over and they finally agreed to take her with them into the forest. It was only through their tolerance of her, as Fossey later acknowledged, that she first met the mountain gorillas.

The morning finally arrived for her adventure—the day she would actually see what has been described as the most spectacular animal in all of Africa. The Roots, along with their gorilla tracker, Sanwekwe, led the way.

Finally, the moment arrived, as Fossey suddenly heard the *wraagh* of a gorilla. Her biographer describes what happened next. "Sanwekwe cut a window in the bush with his panga [machete] and the Roots pushed her forward so she could see [the gorillas] for the first time. She was never the same again."[29]

From that moment on Fossey was totally captivated by these magnificent creatures. Years later she tried to explain the overwhelming compassion she immediately felt toward the animals: "It was their individuality combined with the shyness of their behavior that remained the most captivating impression of this first encounter with the greatest of the great apes."[30]

The next day Fossey reluctantly left Kabara. But she knew, even then, that one day she would return.

A Visit to the Forresters

Before returning to the United States, Fossey flew to Rhodesia to visit Pookie Forrester and his family. While she was there she also met Pookie's older brother Alexie, who stood six feet six inches tall. She was immediately attracted to him. "I think he is inclined to be arrogant," she

From the moment she first saw the mountain gorilla, Fossey was obsessed with working with them. Their huge bulk mixed with their incredible gentleness intrigued Fossey.

later said, "but there's something powerful about him I never felt with Pookie. He's thirty-one, single, and just about the best-looking man I've ever laid eyes on."[31]

Finally, in November 1963, Fossey returned to Louisville and to her mundane existence. She went to work every day at Kosair and even tried to write a few articles about her adventures in Africa. Eventually, three of those articles were published in the *Louisville Courier* newspaper and brought her a bit of celebrity status, at least in Louisville. In one of the articles, titled "I Photographed the Mountain Gorilla," she expressed concern for the future of the mountain gorillas' survival. "How much longer," she wondered, "will they continue to thrive, in view of the many opposing interests threatening their habitat—poachers, agriculturalists, and pastoralists?"[32]

A First Impression

George Schaller describes his first encounter with the mountain gorilla in this excerpt from his book The Year of the Gorilla.

"The musty, somewhat sweet odor of gorilla hung in the air. Somewhere ahead and out of sight, a gorilla roared and roared again, uuuauuua!—an explosive, half-screaming sound that shattered the stillness of the forest and made the hairs on my neck rise. I took a few steps and stopped, listened, and moved again. The only sound was the buzzing of insects. Far below me white clouds crept up the slopes and fingered into the canyons. Then another roar, but farther away. I continued over a ridge, down, and up again. Finally, I saw them, on the opposite slope about two hundred feet away, some sitting on the ground, others in trees. . . . Accustomed to the drab gorillas in zoos . . . I was little prepared for the beauty of the beasts before me."

A Developing Relationship

Soon after her return to the States, Fossey began to correspond with Alexie. In September of the following year, he came to the United States to attend the University of Notre Dame in South Bend, Indiana.

That Thanksgiving he spent a week with Fossey and returned to Louisville for a second visit at Christmas. By early 1965 they decided to get married. But they also decided not to tell anyone about their plans until 1966. Even then, they realized they couldn't get married until the following year, after Alexie graduated from the university.

In the meantime, however, Dr. Louis Leakey arrived in Louisville for a speaking engagement. That single event would change everything for Fossey—forever.

In 1966, three years after she had returned from Africa, Fossey heard that Dr. Leakey was planning to visit the United States on a lecture tour. One of his speaking engagements was at the University of Louisville in Louisville, Kentucky, scheduled for 8:00 P.M. on Sunday, April 3.

Fossey decided to take advantage of the situation and do something that even she couldn't have imagined would so dramatically change her life. That night she grabbed copies of her published newspaper articles and headed for the lecture hall at the university.

After the lecture Fossey went up to speak to the famous scientist. To her amazement, Dr. Leakey actually remembered her and asked if she had ever managed to actually see any mountain gorillas on her trip to Africa. She told him she had and showed him the article called "I Photographed the Mountain Gorilla."

As they talked, Dr. Leakey began to ask Fossey some personal questions. What were her particular interests? What was she planning to do with her life? Would she be interested in returning to Africa someday?

Fossey told Dr. Leakey that what she really wanted to do was to work with animals. She also told him she was especially interested in the gorillas on the Virunga Mountains.

Then Dr. Leakey did something that took Fossey by surprise. He suggested that

she come to see him the next day, adding that she just might be the person he was looking for to head up a long-term research study of the mountain gorillas of the Virungas. Fossey was absolutely astounded—and terribly excited.

Six years earlier Dr. Leakey had raised the money to fund an important study of chimpanzees in the Gombe Stream Research Center in Tanzania. He personally selected Dr. Jane Goodall to conduct the study. Now he was looking for someone like Goodall to head up a long-term study of the almost-extinct mountain gorilla.

An Unlikely Candidate

The next morning Fossey arrived at Dr. Leakey's hotel bright and early—and full of self-doubt. She had any number of reasons why she wasn't qualified for the job Dr. Leakey had in mind for her. First, she told him, she had no money. But Leakey said he would be able to raise the money for the study plus pay her a small salary. In addition, he told her, she would probably be able to earn some money by writing articles for *National Geographic* magazine.

Second, she had no specific educational background for the job. But, again, Leakey brushed that excuse aside. As far as he was concerned, it was better to have someone who had a broad education and who wasn't a primatologist by training, with preset ideas and notions about the animals. As Jane Goodall explains in her first book, *In the Shadow of Man*, "He wanted someone with a mind uncluttered and unbiased by theory, who would make the study for no other reason than a real desire for the knowledge."[33]

Dr. Louis Leakey met with Fossey after her African trip. He eventually would be responsible for funding her first research study of the mountain gorilla.

Finally, Fossey tried one last reason why he shouldn't choose her. She was thirty-four years old. "But this is the perfect age to begin such work," Leakey said. "You have attained maturity and won't be apt to take rash actions."[34] What's more, he added, as far as he was concerned, women were far better suited emotionally to study the great apes than men because he believed women were more patient than men.

So it was settled. In less than an hour, Fossey had become Dr. Leakey's gorilla girl, or, as she later described it, his "intrepid gorilla girl." There was just one other thing.

"Have you had your appendix out?" he asked her. "No," she told him. "I have

not." Dr. Leakey then explained that she should have it removed before she went to Africa. While the request seemed strange, it was, Fossey later explained in her own wry way, "a small sacrifice for such an opportunity."[35]

It was only after the operation that Fossey found out that Dr. Leakey also had a wry (some might say perverse) sense of humor. As he explained in a letter to her, he was just kidding about the need for her to have her appendix out. That was just his way of testing whether an applicant was serious about wanting to do fieldwork in Africa.

On August 1 Fossey left Louisville to visit her parents in California and to wait for word from Dr. Leakey that it was time

---

First Encounter with a Gorilla

Fossey never forgot the moment she first saw the mountain gorilla, which she vividly describes in her book Gorillas in the Mist.

"Sound preceded sight. Odor preceded sound in the form of an overwhelming musky-barnyard, humanlike scent. The air was suddenly rent by a high-pitched series of screams followed by the rhythmic rondo of sharp *pok-pok* chestbeats from a great silverback male. . . . The three of us froze until the echoes of the screams and chestbeats faded. Only then did we slowly creep forward under the cover of dense shrubbery to about fifty feet from the group. Peeking through the vegetation, we could distinguish an equally curious phalanx of black, leather-countenanced, furry-headed primates peering back at us. Their bright eyes darted nervously from under heavy brows as though trying to identify us as familiar friends or possible foes. Immediately I was struck by the physical magnificence of the huge jet-black bodies blended against the green palette wash of the thick forest foliage."

Fossey in 1968. Fossey seemed an unlikely candidate to spend her life in the remote, lonely rain forests of Africa. Frail, young, and plagued by poor health, Fossey would nonetheless conquer her weaknesses to fulfill her life's work.

to go to Africa. For the next four months her parents tried to talk her out of going on such a ridiculous trip. They insisted she was throwing her life away.

Her parents were not the only ones who thought the idea was crazy. In fact, most people thought that the idea of sending a woman with no experience to live on a mountain in Africa was at best preposterous, if not sheer madness.

But Fossey did not care what other people thought. She realized that there was no way she could explain to anyone why she felt such an urgent need to return to Africa. "Some may call it destiny," she later said, "and others may call it dismaying. I call the sudden turn of events in my life fortuitous."[36]

Fossey waited impatiently to hear from Dr. Leakey. At times she almost gave up, thinking that the dream of her life would never become reality. But finally Leakey was able to raise the money to finance the study, and on December 15, 1966, Fossey left on a journey that would change her life forever. She was thirty-four years old.

Chapter

3 From Kentucky to the Congo

Fossey's first stop on her way from the United States to Kisoro, Uganda, in Africa was Heathrow Airport in London. By chance, she ran into the wildlife photographer Joan Root, whom she had met during her first trip to Africa in 1963. Root was on her way to Nairobi, which was also Fossey's next stop on her journey to the Congo.

Fossey told Root about her plans to begin a two-year study of the mountain gorilla. She explained to Root that she planned to conduct her research study from Kabara Meadow on Mount Mikeno in the Congo, the same site that Schaller had used as his base of operations seven years earlier.

Root was incredulous, particularly when Fossey explained that she intended to carry out this research study virtually by herself. Once they arrived in Nairobi, Root helped Fossey shop for the various camping supplies and equipment she would need during her stay on the mountain. Fossey also bought a jeep that she promptly named Lily.

Dr. Leakey had arranged for Fossey to spend a couple of days with Jane Goodall at the Gombe Stream Reserch Center in Tanzania. There, Goodall taught Fossey some methods of camp organization and data collecting. But, as Fossey later recalled, "I fear that I was not an apprecia-

tive guest, for I was desperately keen to reach Kabara and the mountain gorillas."[37]

After returning once again to Nairobi, Fossey learned that Leakey had asked pho-

Jane Goodall at Gombe Stream Research Center in Tanzania. Goodall's work with chimps preceded Fossey's.

tographer Alan Root to accompany her to the Congo. Root graciously agreed. So, after the Christmas holidays Fossey and Root set out for the long drive from Nairobi, Kenya, to Kisoro, Uganda—just five miles from the Congo. Root led the way in his jeep, and Fossey followed in Lily.

When they arrived in Kisoro, they went immediately to the Traveller's Rest, where Fossey was once again delighted to meet Walter Baumgartel. Baumgartel, however, was not so pleased to see her when he heard that she and Root were on their way to the Congo. "I was shocked and dismayed," he says, "when the two told me that they were on their way to that country." "This is madness," he said. The Congo was undergoing a great deal of political upheaval and turmoil. "How could Dr. Leakey even think about sending this American woman to the Congo at a time when most of the whites have fled?" he wondered.[38] But Fossey was unmoved. Nothing was going to stop her from getting to Kabara.

Dian examines a gorilla track. Fossey became adept at tracking the gorilla, carefully scanning the rain forest paths for broken twigs and branches, scat, and footprints.

A New Home at Kabara

Fossey and Root arrived at the small village of Kibumba at the base of Mount Mikeno on January 6, 1967, just a few days before Fossey's thirty-fifth birthday. In Kibumba they hired several porters to help carry their supplies and then began the long and difficult climb up nearly four thousand feet to Kabara Meadow.

Once there, Alan Root put up a tent for Fossey. It measured seven by ten feet and became, as Fossey put it, "a combined bedroom, office, bath, and drying area for my clothes, constantly wet in the rain for-est climate."[39] This tent would be her home for the first few months of her stay there. Later, she would move into a two-room cabin that was only slightly bigger than her tent.

The day after they arrived at Kabara, Fossey learned her first lesson in tracking gorillas. Root had found some gorilla tracks, so in her enthusiasm to find the gorillas, Fossey immediately set out to follow them. After a few minutes of tracking, however, she suddenly realized that Root wasn't behind her. So she backtracked until she found him still sitting at the same place where they first found the tracks. "Dian," he told her, "if you are ever going to contact gorillas, you must follow their tracks to where they are going rather than

Sanwekwe, a tracker who taught Fossey a great deal about how to find the reclusive animals.

backtrack trails to where they've been."[40] It was a lesson she would never forget.

The next day Alan Root left. Looking back on that day, Fossey said, "I felt a sense of panic while watching Alan fade into the foliage near the descending edge of the Kabara meadow. He was my last link with civilization as I had always known it."[41]

Soon after Alan Root departed, the tracker Sanwekwe arrived. Sanwekwe was an experienced tracker, having worked with George Schaller in 1960 and more recently for Joan and Alan Root, and he taught Fossey a great deal. She quickly learned that following gorilla tracks is, in fact, rather easy. She learned, for example, that most vegetation "bends in the direction of a group's travel, knuckleprints may be found impressed upon intermittent dirt patches or trails, and chains of gorilla dung deposits provide other clues as to the direction of the animals' passage."[42]

During that time Fossey also learned a great deal about living in the rain forests of the Virungas, which, at times, must have seemed like living at the very end of the earth. Once a month she would go to Kisoro, Uganda, a two-hour drive from the base of Mount Mikeno, for supplies. She would stock up on "cans of hot dogs, Spam, powdered milk, margarine, corned beef, tuna, hash, and various vegetables, as well as boxes of noodles, spaghetti, oatmeal, and bags of sweets."[43]

Perhaps the most important thing she had learned, however, was to "accept the animals on their own terms and never to push them beyond the varying levels of tolerance they were willing to give." As she would often point out in later years, "Any observer is an intruder in the domain of a wild animal and must remember that the rights of that animal supersede human interests."[44]

Her Methods of Research

From the beginning Fossey had decided she wanted to make her study of the mountain gorillas different from George Schaller's famous study. Schaller had stud-

Mountain Gorilla Groups

Mountain gorillas live in family groups. In her book, Gorillas in the Mist, *Dian Fossey describes a typical group.*

"A typical group contains: one silverback, a sexually mature male over the age of fifteen years, who is the group's undisputed leader and weighs roughly 375 pounds, or about twice the size of a female; one blackjack, a sexually immature male between eight and thirteen years weighing some 253 pounds; three to four sexually mature females over eight years, each about 200 pounds, who are ordinarily bonded to the dominant silverback for life; and, lastly, from three to six immature members, those under eight years. Immatures were divided into young adults between six and eight years, weighing about 170 pounds each, juveniles between three and six years, weighing some 120 pounds, and infants, from birth to three years, weighing between 2 and 30 pounds."

One of Fossey's first experiences with mountain gorillas was to survive the headlong charge of a huge male silverback. Cautioned to remain absolutely still, Fossey survived the charge and learned from it.

ied range behavior of the mountain gorilla. He observed what they ate, where they slept at night, and how they occupied their time during the day. He also observed the mountain gorillas mainly from a distance and didn't try to habituate them or interact with them.

So Fossey decided she wanted to study social behavior—the social dynamics within the groups and how they interacted with one another. She wanted to learn more about the gorillas' diet and what they would eat and not eat; and she

A family group of mountain gorillas in their natural habitat. Fossey was fascinated by the social habits of the huge creatures, finding that many of their habits were surprisingly humanlike.

wanted to study their mating habits in order to learn more about reproduction. In general, she wanted to have intimate and personal contact with the gorillas. And in order to do that, she had to habituate the gorillas, get them used to her presence, and eventually try to interact with them.

At first, she tried to make the mountain gorillas comfortable with her presence by talking softly to them. But that seemed to merely frighten them more. So, she decided to act like a gorilla. As she later explained:

> I learned to scratch and groom and beat my chest. I imitated my subject's vocalizations (hoots, grunts, and belches), munched the foliage they ate, kept low to the ground and deliberate in movement—in short, showed that my curiosity about them matched theirs toward me.[45]

By imitating their eating, grooming, and vocalization habits, Fossey was eventually able to get these extraordinarily strong but amazingly shy and gentle animals to respond favorably to her. She freely admitted, however, that her methods were not always dignified. "One feels a fool thumping one's chest rhythmically," she confessed, "or sitting about pretending to munch on a stalk of wild celery as though it were the most delectable morsel in the world."[46]

The Sounds of a Gorilla

Early in her study Fossey decided that the best way to habituate the gorillas was to imitate the sounds or vocalizations that they made, and eventually she identified twenty-

To be accepted by the gorillas, Fossey attempted to imitate their behaviors. To prevent the gorillas from feeling threatened, Fossey would lay low to the ground in a submissive position.

five distinct sounds. But three sounds were most common and she used these most frequently. She called one of these sounds the belch vocalization because gorillas used it usually when they were eating or when they were very content. It was a soft purring vocalization that sounded like "naooom, naooom, naooom."

A second common sound was called the hoot bark, which gorillas used whenever they were alarmed or curious about something. Finally, there was the pig grunt, a harsh staccato sound that the gorillas normally used when they were disciplining their youngsters and infants.

It was the belch vocalization, however, that Fossey came to use most often herself.

Since this vocalization was a sign of contentment among the gorillas, Fossey repeated it whenever she approached a gorilla group. It was her way of letting them know that everything was okay, that there was no need to be alarmed.

Bluff Charges

Before coming to Kabara Meadow, Fossey had read a book that Schaller wrote called *The Year of the Gorilla.* It told about his experiences observing gorillas a few years earlier. In it Schaller said that gorillas rarely charge at people. If they do, he

Relating to Gorillas

Walter Baumgartel believes that Fossey was so successful with the gorillas because she could relate to them in a very natural and nonthreatening way, as he illustrates in this excerpt from his book Up Among the Mountain Gorillas.

"Dian [was] not an expert at climbing trees. One day a group of gorillas watched her try to get hold of a low branch to pull herself up to a vantage point. As she clung to the branch, intermittently dangling and falling back to the ground, the gorillas seemed to be enjoying her performance. For the first time, instead of fleeing, they gave way to their curiosity and approached within twenty feet to sit and stare at her clumsiness. To humor them, Dian prolonged her struggle and let herself fall several times. No wonder the gorillas began to like her and lose their fear of the strange, awkward creature."

said, they are generally just bluffing. It is called a bluff charge. If a gorilla starts to charge, Schaller warned, it's important, if not critical, not to run. Rather, you should stand perfectly still.

At first Fossey found this advice rather difficult to follow, even though she firmly believed in the gentle nature of gorillas. Nevertheless, as she once explained it, "because of the intensity of their screams and the speed of their approaches, I found it possible to face charging gorillas only by clinging to surrounding vegetation for dear life. Without that support, I surely would have turned tail and run."[47]

Once she was climbing through tall vegetation on the side of the mountain when she suddenly heard the deafening roar of a group of five male gorillas charging toward her. The lead silverback got within three feet of Fossey, when he abruptly stopped, which caused the other four gorillas to fall over him. Fossey immediately sank to the ground in an important

submissive position. For the next half hour, she lay on the ground, listening to the gorillas scream every time she made the slightest move. She also heard the voices of a group of Watusi herdsmen coming toward her.

Finally the gorillas moved away. She later learned that the Watusi had been convinced that she must have been torn to shreds by the gorillas. But when they saw her stand up, they were astonished. After that, they believed she had a special kind of magic power, called *sumu*. Years later she would use her *sumu* to help protect the mountain gorillas.

A Revolution and Expulsion

On July 9, 1967, Fossey's research on Mount Mikeno came to a sudden and abrupt end. She had spent most of the day in the forests, observing her gorillas. When she returned to camp at 3:30 P.M., she discovered armed soldiers waiting for her.

They handed her a letter from Anicet Mburanumwe, the director of the Parc National des Virungas. His letter told her that there was a civil war going on in Zaire, the new name for the Congo. For her own safety, he said, she must leave Kabara Meadow immediately.

The guards escorted Fossey to the park headquarters at Rumangabo. At first Fossey was not too concerned. But by the end of the first week, she learned that the border between Zaire and Uganda was closed, and she suddenly realized that she might not ever get out of the country. So she devised a plan to escape.

Fossey learned that the guards were going to confiscate her jeep, since it was not properly registered. But Fossey convinced the guards that she had money in Kisoro, Uganda—almost $400—that she would give them to register the car in Zaire. But first she had to get the money.

"The enticement of that much cash," she later wrote, "along with the anticipated acquisition of the car as well as a cooperative hostage, was too much for the soldiers to resist. They agreed to 'escort' me to Uganda under armed guard."[48]

A Lucky Escape

As soon as Fossey and the armed guards crossed the border into Uganda, Fossey headed for the Traveller's Rest Inn. It was there, she told the guards, she would be able to get the money. But when she arrived at the hotel, she suddenly darted inside, ran into one of the bedrooms, and hid under the bed. Walter Baumgartel,

the owner of the hotel, called the Ugandan police to arrest the Zairean soldiers.

A few days later Fossey flew to Nairobi, where she met with Dr. Leakey. It was only then that she learned just how serious the situation in Zaire really was. It was so serious, in fact, that the U.S. Department of State had declared her "missing and assumed dead."

Fossey's encounter with the huge silverback that charged her but did not harm her caused rumors among the rain forest natives that she possessed sumu, *or magical powers.*

Fossey, next to her jeep, Lily, hires porters to carry her supplies into the rain forest to set up a permanent camp. While being detained at park headquarters during the civil war in Zaire, Fossey devised a successful plan of escape and managed to prevent the confiscation of her jeep.

Fossey was happy and relieved that she had escaped. But her research was clearly not finished. She would now have to find a new place to conduct her research on the mountain gorillas. That place, she decided, would be the tiny country of Rwanda. She could study the mountain gorillas from the Rwandan side of the Virunga volcanoes.

Once arrangements were made for her to go to Rwanda, she was elated. As she put it, "There still were gorillas to find and mountains to climb. It was like being reborn."[49]

Chapter

4 A New Beginning

Known as the Land of a Thousand Hills, Rwanda is one of the smallest and poorest countries in Africa. With only 10,136 square miles, Rwanda is about the size of the state of Maryland. Yet, with seven million people, it has one and one-half times the population of Maryland.

Most of the people who live in Rwanda are members of one of three groups. The Hutu (or Bahutu) make up 85 percent of all the people in Rwanda and are farmers. The Tutsi (or Watusi) make up about 14 percent of the population and are cattle herders. The Twa (or Batwa) make up 1 percent of the population, and are hunters and honey gatherers.

For hundreds of years these groups had used the Virungas for hunting or for cattle grazing. Then, in 1929, the Albert National Park was established as a sanctuary for wildlife. Technically and legally, that meant that the parkland was off-limits to hunters and cattle grazers.

Yet over the years little was done to enforce the law and Rwandan hunters continued to use the parkland illegally to hunt duiker, buffalo, and other animals, while the farmers continued to graze their cattle in the protected area.

These two groups—the hunters and the cattle grazers—would soon become Fossey's hated enemies, since both groups

Mount Karisimbi in Rwanda. Fossey would set up a permanent camp between Mounts Karasimbi and Visoke.

posed a serious threat to the survival of the mountain gorillas. Yet, for now, Fossey's first task in Rwanda was to set up a new research station.

Searching for a New Home

As soon as Fossey arrived in Rwanda, she went immediately to the American embassy. Even though embassy officials were skeptical about finding gorillas in Rwanda, they suggested she talk with another American woman named Rosamond Carr, who owned a farm outside of Gisenyi.

On July 20, 1967, Fossey sent a note to Carr, asking to see her the next day. She explained to Carr that she had been working on the Congo side of Mount Karisimbi, but was recently expelled from the country. She now wanted to continue her research on the Rwanda side of Karisimbi.

Carr had lived in Rwanda for more than thirty years and was convinced there were no gorillas in the Parc National des Volcans. But she agreed to talk with Fossey anyway.

Years later, Carr recalled her first impressions of this fiercely determined, young American woman. "I was impressed by the tall attractive girl wearing a lovely lilac dress with dirty tennis shoes (the shoes she had on when she fled from Zaire)," Carr recalled. "Her dark hair was worn in a thick braid over one shoulder and her brown eyes were appraising and rather startling."[50]

At lunch that day Carr told Fossey that she was certain no gorillas lived on her side of Karisimbi. But Fossey refused to believe that. The Rwandan side of the Virungas was only a few miles from Kabara Meadow.

How could the gorillas know there was a border between the two countries?

Finally, Carr told Fossey that Alyette De-Munck, a woman who owned a farm just a mile or two down the road from Carr at the base of Mount Karisimbi, might know something more. DeMunck had grown up in Zaire, but had recently moved to Rwanda. Like Fossey, she was an adventurer who knew a great deal about the Virungas.

Soon afterward DeMunck and Fossey met and the two hit it off immediately. De-Munck agreed to help Fossey and let her use her plantation near Karisimbi as a base of operations while she explored the forests of Mount Karisimbi, searching for the right campsite.

Fossey's search was discouraging, because what she discovered throughout the

Alyette DeMunck helps Fossey with her new cabin. DeMunck had a farm not too far from where Dian would make her first study of the gorilla.

Hiking Through the Virungas

A trip into the forest to search for the gorilla groups was physically exhausting. This description is taken from a Discover *magazine article by Wayne McGuire.*

"The hike through the forest can be grueling. In some places you have to crawl on your belly. When you walk, the heavy vegetation can wrap around your ankle and—whoosh!—you're on your face. You also have to contend with giant stinging nettles. Some burn and some itch; I much prefer the latter. The first day I went out in the field . . . we went into Zaire, which is loaded with giant stinging nettles, and when we got back, I was sore from the neck down."

Fossey moves through patches of her nemesis, the stinging nettle. Fossey was remarkable in her ability to withstand the discomforts of rain forest living.

park were illegal cattle herders and hunters, but no gorillas. One day, however, while surveying the mountainside with binoculars, Fossey spotted a likely area between Mount Karisimbi and Mount Visoke. Instinctively, she knew she had found her new home.

Establishing Karisoke

On September 24, 1967, Fossey set out to climb Mount Visoke, along with Alyette DeMunck and several dozen porters, all comfortably carrying boxes of supplies on top of their heads. Several hours later this unusual team came to a broad meadow that forms part of the saddle area connecting Mount Karisimbi, Mount Mikeno, and Mount Visoke. It was here at precisely 4:30 P.M. that Dian Fossey established the Karisoke Research Centre. She named the center by combining the names of two of the mountains—the first four letters from Karisimbi and the last four letters from Visoke. Fossey said years later:

Fossey and porters carry supplies to the remote Karisoke Research Centre.

Little did I know then that by setting up two small tents in the wilderness of the Virungas I had launched the beginnings of what was to become an internationally renowned research station eventually to be utilized by students and scientists from many countries.[51]

She had also established what would become her home for the rest of her life.

On the day that Karisoke was established, two Batwa poachers had been hunting duiker on the slopes of Mount Visoke when they heard gorillas. They knew of the strange American woman who was planning to study these huge animals, so they went to her camp, and offered to lead her to the fourteen-member group.

Fossey was ecstatic. Yet, she was also troubled by the presence of poachers in the new Karisoke study area. As biographer Farley Mowat explains in his book *Woman in the Mists*, she was "hard-pressed to decide whether to run the poachers out of camp or accept their offer. In the end she followed them to the gorillas, but issued a stern warning that from this day forward neither cattle herding nor poaching would be tolerated in her part of the park."[52]

A few days later Alyette DeMunck left Karisoke and Fossey suddenly found herself alone with a group of Rwandans who spoke only Kinyarwanda, the language of Rwanda, while she, at best, spoke only a little Swahili. Suddenly, the reality of the situation must have sunk in. Here she was, a white woman alone on a mountain with a group of men who spoke a language she could not understand. She was so terrified that when a porter came up to speak to her, she ran inside her tent to hide. Later she learned he only wanted to know if she needed some hot water. Despite her anxiety, she remained determined to succeed.

A Visit from Alexie

On October 9 Alexie Forrester arrived at Karisoke to try to talk Fossey into leaving the mountain. Not only did he want to marry her, but he was also afraid for her safety. As he put it, "It was absolutely ludicrous to live on a mountain out there, harassing a bunch of poachers and expecting to stay alive."[53]

For the next five days Fossey and Forrester talked about her work with the gorillas and her safety. And they talked about their relationship. Forrester pleaded with Fossey to come to her senses and return with him to the United States, where he was still a student. But Fossey refused. She was determined to continue her work with the mountain gorillas. He then offered to stay with her at Karisoke for a year while she completed her study of the gorillas if she would then return with him. Once again she refused.

Finally Forrester gave Fossey an ultimatum. Either return to the United States immediately and marry, or forget about ever getting married—at least to him. For the third and final time she declined his proposal.

When it became clear that Fossey was not going to abandon her research, Forrester offered her some advice. He was afraid for her life, afraid she would get her throat cut by poachers. But there was one way she might survive. He told her she had to turn herself into a spiritual witch. "I suggested she should make herself into someone no one would want to go *near*— that she should get wailing systems, smoke bombs, false faces, that sort of thing. And

I told her to leave these things lying about everywhere, and to make sure everybody knew they were there."[54] When Forrester finally left Karisoke, he was convinced that Fossey would be murdered before the year was out.

During her many years at Karisoke, Fossey took Forrester's advice. As Mary Smith of the National Geographic Society in Washington, D.C., recalls, "She would go to the stores here when she was in town and buy up beads, firecrackers, and Halloween masks. She literally hoped to scare the poachers to death."[55]

Life in the Virungas

From the beginning Fossey loved Karisoke. And no wonder. "Karisoke is a beautiful place," one former student says, "with tall, ancient hagenia trees scattered throughout the clearing."[56] It was also a place where she was surrounded by animals of all kinds from water buffalo to antelope to elephants. In addition, she acquired a number of pets, including a bulldog named Cindy and a small blue monkey named Kima.

But living at Karisoke, ten thousand feet up on a volcanic mountain, was not so easy. Nearly every day it would rain, making it extremely difficult to get around. As one writer who has visited Karisoke explains:

> Even on sunny days the slopes are difficult—slippery, wet, and tangled. . . . It is almost impossible to walk anywhere without cutting a trail with a machete, and every step is a side-heaving struggle up 45-degree slopes. Fields of nettles deliver a punishing sting that feels like electric needles even through two layers of clothing.[57]

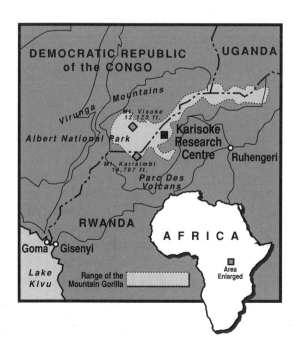

Fossey loved animals and Karisoke was soon full of them. Pictured are her dog, Cindy, and pet monkey, Kima (left). (Below) From the start, Fossey ran afoul of poachers because of her relentless endeavors to free animals such as this duiker from their traps.

Of course, there were always dangers in the field. As she searched for the gorillas, she would have to watch out for traps set for duikers. These nooses would occasionally catch gorillas, cutting deeply into their ankles or wrists, often leaving them with gangrene. They could just as easily catch human beings.

The terrain itself was rugged and often dangerous. Once Fossey fell into a ditch while trying to avoid a charging buffalo and broke her ankle.

Pit traps were another danger. These were holes that were dug six to eight feet deep and covered over with vegetation. At the bottom of the trap, the poachers placed sharply pointed bamboo stakes. The stakes, which pointed straight up, were designed to impale any animal who fell into the pit.

Once Fossey herself fell into one of these pits. Fortunately, the pit was old and the stakes had rotted, so she wasn't seriously injured. As she looked up the side of the eight-foot deep hole, she wondered for a moment how she would get out. Typical of Fossey's sardonic sense of humor, she later noted, "This was one of the very few times in my life when I was grateful for my six-foot height."[58]

There was another danger in living almost totally isolated from traditional American civilization. After a while Fossey seemed to forget many of the common procedures or acceptable habits of modern life. Once she announced at a conference that the most difficult thing to remember in America was to flush the toilet. At another time she went to dinner with some young students and without thinking nonchalantly started to lick pats of butter off the cardboard backings. As one student explained it, "A lot of people get strange up here. It's the loneliness that is hardest to cope with. You forget how to speak English, forget how to interact with humans."[59]

Despite the hardships, however, Fossey considered herself the luckiest person in the world. "When contemplating the vast expanse of uninhabited, rugged, mountainous land surrounding me and such a wealth of wilderness for my backyard, I considered myself one of the world's most fortunate people," she said.[60]

Relationships

Throughout her life, Fossey was torn between her total dedication to her work and animals and her desire to have a real home and family and children. But as one former student explains, "Her trouble with relationships was that she could never give herself completely; she always pulled back because she wanted to keep her independence."[61]

In August 1968 *National Geographic* magazine sent wildlife photographer Bob Campbell to shoot some film of Fossey and her gorillas. From then until the spring of 1972, Campbell lived at Karisoke almost full-time.

At first Fossey did not care for Campbell. But eventually the two became romantically involved, even though Campbell maintains that he never really fell in love with Fossey. "They were lovers," says biographer Harold Hayes, "but their behavior was restrained and detached."[62]

Nevertheless, most people agree that the years that Bob Campbell spent at Karisoke were the best years of Fossey's

life. During that time he helped Fossey with anti-poaching patrols, helped train new staff members at the camp, and served as a general handyman.

Campbell's assignment was to capture Fossey on film with the gorillas. But Fossey made it very difficult for him to film the gorillas. According to Campbell:

> She tied me down to her standard methods of observation. She wouldn't have me harassing the animals or doing things to make them react; just go out, find them, sit in a good observation spot and then watch what they do. I wasn't to follow them around.[63]

In the end, after three years, Campbell had very little footage of Fossey and the gorillas.

Fossey became romantically involved with Bob Campbell, the National Geographic *photographer sent to Karisoke in 1968 to capture footage of Fossey and the gorillas.*

One of Bob Campbell's photos shows Fossey at work with the gorillas.

Education

By fall of 1968 Fossey knew she needed a break. It had been almost sixteen months since she arrived in Africa, and she was becoming, as she put it, "bushy." What's more, she was having a great deal of trouble with her teeth and she desperately needed to see a dentist.

At the same time, Fossey began to realize that she needed to go back to school. Although her work with the mountain gorillas had become fairly well known throughout the scientific community, she knew that in order for her work to be taken seriously, she would need to get a doctorate. "Without that Big Degree," she often said, "you don't cut much ice no matter how good you are."[64]

On September 24, 1968, Fossey left Karisoke to return to the United States for the first time in almost two years. On her way she stopped off in England to meet Professor Robert Hinde, head of graduate studies in animal behavior at Cambridge

University, and to discuss a doctoral program. It would not be until January 1970, however, that Fossey finally would begin her course work at Cambridge. For the next four years she would return to Cambridge for three to six months at a time to complete the required courses. During all

In 1968, Fossey left Karisoke for Cambridge University to earn a doctorate. She hated having to return to civilization, constantly longing for the mountains and her gorillas.

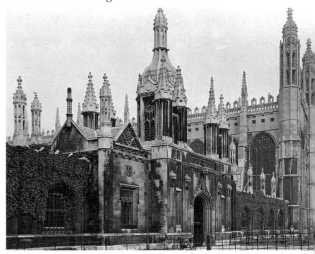

The Pleasures of the Virungas

George Schaller, in Gorilla: Struggle for Survival in the Virungas, *quotes David Watts, one of Fossey's students describing life in the Virungas.*

"Evenings are quiet, except for the unearthly shrieking of the hyrax. That is the time when the solitude and the simplicity of life there closes in. It is not a way of life that many Westerners would desire, but it brings immense rewards to those who can endure the solitude without undue difficulty. It offers a chance to learn about the world and our place in it, both personally and collectively. The pleasure and privilege of knowing the gorillas and watching their lives is like nothing else in the world."

Bob Campbell views the peaceful Virunga Mountains.

of that time she never really liked being at Cambridge. "I hate it here because it isn't Africa," she told Leakey. "I feel like a mole."[65]

Nevertheless, she stuck to it and finally, in May 1976, she became Dr. Fossey. She had not only won her doctorate in zoology, she had also won the right to demand respect from the scientific community.

Yet, in the summer of 1968, as Fossey flew home to the United States for the first time in almost two years, all of that was still to come. Now she simply wanted to take care of her teeth and visit some old friends.

She also went to California to visit her parents, who still could not understand her choice of career. They pleaded with her to return home. Why was she throwing her life away in Africa? they asked. Why couldn't she return home where she belonged? These were questions they would continue to ask Fossey throughout the rest of her life. But by now, for Dian Fossey, home was thousands of miles away on a mountain in Africa.

Chapter

5 Poachers and Cattle Herders

Early in her work at Karisoke, Fossey predicted that poachers and cattle herders would have a significant effect on her life and on the lives of the gorillas in her study groups. She couldn't have been more right.

Cattle were a problem on the Virungas because they trampled the vegetation that provided food for the mountain gorillas. As Fossey once explained to her friend Rosamond Carr:

> The herders ruin the habitat. . . . They keep ten times what they need, just for prestige. There are so many up here now—they churn the ground until it

looks as if it were plowed. They crush the plants the gorillas eat, shut them out of the best feeding areas, and force them higher and higher up the slopes into the cold and wet until they get pneumonia.[66]

Destructive Hunters

Fossey would tirelessly travel around the Karisoke study area driving cattle out. Yet the cattle herds were not nearly as destructive as the poachers.

One of Fossey's African workers drives cattle from the preserve. Fossey became infuriated by such illegal grazing.

Some of the poachers were trophy hunters. For a while in the 1970s there was a strong market among some tourists for the head or hand of a gorilla. Poachers would kill gorillas and sell the heads or hands as souvenirs. An ashtray made from a gorilla hand was a popular item among some tourists at one time.

The biggest threat to the mountain gorillas at this time, however, came from foreign zoos that would pay poachers to capture infant gorillas. Because gorilla groups have a strong family bond and protect their young at any cost, the poachers would have to kill the silverbacks and the mothers in order to get the babies.

From the time she first arrived in Rwanda, Fossey constantly complained to the park authorities about the cattle herders and poachers. She wanted the Rwanda Office of Tourism and National Parks to increase patrols by armed guards to drive herders and their cattle out of the park. She even tried to get help from the Rwandan government in the capital, Kigali. Yet, according to one of her biographers, "she was received with total indifference. The gorillas were good for nothing; they served no purpose for the people of Rwanda, most of whom had never seen them and were scarcely aware they were there."[67]

Fossey's War

The result was that Fossey waged war against the cattle herders and the poachers by herself. And she did so with an increasing vengeance, even though she understood how important all land was to

---

Active Versus Theoretical Conservation

Early in her career as a primatologist, Fossey became an advocate of what she called active conservation. In this excerpt from her book Gorillas in the Mist, *she explains the difference between active and theoretical conservation.*

"Active conservation includes frequent patrols in wildlife areas to destroy poacher equipment and weapons, firm and prompt law enforcement, census counts in regions of breeding and ranging concentration, and strong safeguards for the limited habitat the animals occupy . . . [and the] enforcement of anti-encroacher laws as well as severe penalties for the illegal sale of poached animals for their meat, skins, tusks, or for financial profits. . . . Theoretical conservation seeks to encourage growth in tourism by improving existing roads that circle the mountains of the Parc des Volcans, by renovating the park headquarters and tourists' lodging, and by the habituation of gorillas near the park boundaries for tourists to visit and photograph."

Dian's tactics against poachers and herdsmen were dangerously direct. Here she destroys a cattle herder's shed illegally located in the park. To protect herself, Fossey cultivated the natives' notion that she was a witch.

Rwandans for farming or hunting—even the land in the protected park area.

Land for farming or hunting in Rwanda is scarce. For some of the people in Rwanda, the only way to make a living for their families is to use the protected park preserve for hunting and cattle grazing. Many Rwandans say this is fair because the land has been used in that way for generations upon generations. It is part of their tradition to hunt in the rain forests of the Virungas. What right, they ask, does anyone have to interfere—particularly a white woman from America?

To a certain extent Fossey agreed with them. "Africa belongs to the Africans," she would sometimes say. And at those moments, she would even ask herself what right she had to tell the Watusi to take their cattle outside the park boundaries or to tell the Twa that they could not hunt there.

Yet, invariably, she would come back to the same conclusion. The park had to be protected in order to save the mountain gorillas from extinction. The fact that the Rwandan people needed the land to feed their families did not justify destroying the thirty thousand acres of the Parc des Volcans—all of which occupied only half of 1 percent of all of Rwanda anyway. Her reasoning went like this:

> Each year another 23,000 Rwandese families need additional land for cultivation. Even if the entire park were given over for agricultural purposes, it would provide land for only one quarter of one year's increase in Rwanda's population. This cultivation would, of course, mean total annihilation of the mountain gorilla and other wildlife now trying to survive there, as well as the destruction of the rain forest upon which people and wildlife in Rwanda depend in order to live.[68]

Questionable Tactics

Consequently, Fossey concluded that the park laws had to be strictly enforced to save the mountain gorillas from extinction. There simply wasn't any other option. And she would enforce those laws, even if nobody else did.

Food Versus the Mountain Gorillas

Despite her war against poachers, Fossey also seemed to understand why many people in Rwanda might resent the gorillas' sanctuary, as she explains in her book Gorillas in the Mist.

"Foreigners cannot expect the average Rwandan living near the boundaries of the Parc des Volcans and raising pyrethrum [chrysanthemums] for the equivalent of four cents a pound to look around at the towering volcanoes, consider their majestic beauty, and express concern about an endangered animal species living in those misted mountains. Much as a European might see a mirage when stranded in a desert, a Rwandan sees rows upon rows of potatoes, beans, peas, corn, and tobacco in place of the massive *Hagenia* trees. He justifiably resents being refused access to parkland for realization of his vision."

Poaching, in Fossey's mind, was not only illegal, it was immoral. Yet, over the years, her own aggressive methods for preventing poaching gradually became, according to many reports, both illegal and immoral. For example, once when poachers had kidnapped her dog Cindy, Fossey retaliated by taking eight Tutsi cattle as hostage. She then let it be known that she would kill one cow a day until her dog was returned. She got it back by nightfall.

Once she even went to a notorious poacher's home to attempt to capture him by herself. Finding that he was gone, she went into a rage, trying to find his gun:

> She tore down the matting from the walls inside the hut, dragged it outside, and set it afire. She demanded that the wives give her the gun and grabbed one of his children, a four-year-old boy, threatening to hurt him if they didn't obey.[69]

Dian with her dog, Cindy. When Cindy was kidnapped by poachers in retaliation for Fossey's tactics against them, Fossey threatened to kill native cows until Cindy was safely returned.

Witchcraft

Many Africans believe in witchcraft, or *sumu*. In fact, when Fossey first climbed Mount Karisimbi in search of a new location for her research station, she discovered many signs of *sumu*:

> crossed sticks leading to poachers' traps, which signified death to anyone who tampered with them; buried animal ribs that reputedly could kill meddlers; poisons that her African staff believed would cause them to waste away unless the local witch doctor could provide an antidote.[70]

Almost from the beginning of her work at Karisoke, Fossey took advantage of the Africans' belief in witchcraft. She wanted to make the poachers and cattle herders believe that she had supernatural or magical powers. "She painted hexes, cast spells, pronounced curses," says Sy Montgomery in her book *Walking with the Great Apes*. "'I am the Goddess of the Mountain,' she would hiss in KiSwahili, 'and I will avenge you for killing my children.'"[71]

Many people who knew Fossey at that time grew concerned about her use of witchcraft. Some say she started to believe in her own supernatural powers. Others were simply concerned about what might happen if the Africans ever realized that she didn't really have magical powers. "I used to think that if the natives ever caught on that she wasn't supernatural," says Mary Smith of the National Geographic Society, "they'd attack her."[72]

By the late 1970s Fossey spent almost all of her time fighting poachers and leading anti-poaching patrols. During these patrols she would confiscate poachers' weapons, burn their camps and their houses, and destroy their traps. She reportedly even paid the park guards to bring her captured poachers for interrogation and then would pistol-whip the captives to make them name other poachers. "Dian Fossey was to gorillas what Greenpeace is to whales," says Ian Redmond, a wildlife biologist and former student at Karisoke.[73]

In later years, when she was too ill to go on patrols herself, she hired men to patrol the Parc des Volcans. She also urged Rwandan officials to authorize these

---

Dealing with Poachers

Fossey's method of dealing with poachers was notorious, as this excerpt from a letter quoted in Walking with the Great Apes *illustrates.*

"We stripped him and spread eagled him outside my cabin and lashed the holy blue sweat out of him with nettle stalks and leaves, concentrating on the places where it might hurt a mite. . . . I then went through the ordinary 'sumu,' black magic routine of Mace, ether, needles and masks, ended with sleeping pills. . . . That is called 'conservation'—not talk."

To counter poaching, Fossey set up patrols using natives and students who worked at the center. During these patrols, snares and weapons were seized and brought back to camp. Fossey detested poachers because she had seen the terrible consequences of their work.

armed patrols to kill the poachers, if necessary. As far as Fossey was concerned, poachers should be shown no mercy. "I definitely advocate giving the Conservator and qualified Park guards full license to kill on sight any poachers fleeing when encountered within the interior of the Park," she once wrote.[74] She felt her position was totally justified. There were only a few hundred mountain gorillas left. If drastic measures were not taken to protect them, they would soon be extinct.

Human Encroachment

But it was not just the poachers and cattle herders that incurred Fossey's wrath. She also abhorred what she called human encroachment, whether it was by foreign tourists or Rwandans themselves. Rwandan encroachment involved their continual need for more farmland. Tourists, on the other hand, were an entirely different problem—particularly those who did not respect the land or the gorillas. Once, according to Fossey, a French film team "relentlessly pursued Group 5 [a group of gorillas] daily for six weeks."[75] The trauma of the pursuit, Fossey maintains, caused one of the pregnant females in Group 5 to abort.

Some people charged that Fossey's approach to protecting the gorillas could even be called racist, since she refused to let the gorillas become habituated to her African staff and even tried to prevent local blacks, including the president of

Fossey meets up with her first gorilla tracker Sanwekwe (center) and other ranger patrol guards. Fossey advocated drastic measures against poachers, believing that Park guards should be authorized to kill poachers on sight.

Rwanda, from visiting the gorillas. Fossey explained her viewpoint this way. "Gorillas have known Africans only as poachers in the past. The second that it takes a gorilla to determine if an African is friend or foe is the second that might cost the animal its life from a spear, arrow, or bullet."[76]

Looking back on that time, Alan Goodall, one of Fossey's students, says:

> We had become judge, jury and jailer about park management in Rwanda. . . . It was as though Rwanda had become our own private empire, with no sense of responsibility on our part to those in-

volved. . . . I had the feeling after I left that the African people wanted to see all the gorillas killed so that all of us would leave.[77]

Fossey was determined to do whatever was necessary to protect the gorillas and to keep the gorillas' enemies—cattle herders, poachers, tourists, or government officials—out of the Parc des Volcans and away from *her* gorillas, even if it meant taking the law into her own hands. It was this unswerving determination that would eventually cause her to lose for a while the very thing she loved most.

6 The Study Groups at Karisoke

When Fossey first began her study of the mountain gorillas at Kabara, Zaire's Parc National des Virungas was well protected from poachers. Consequently, the gorillas there were not particularly afraid of her presence. As a result, during her six-month stay in this part of the Virungas, she was able to quickly make contact with three gorilla groups and to habituate them rather easily.

At Karisoke, however, the situation was vastly different. Rwanda's Parc National des Volcans was not well protected and the gorillas there had been confronted repeatedly by both poachers and cattle herdsmen. As a result, the gorillas were initially far more reluctant to accept Fossey.

Nevertheless, during the first two years at Karisoke, Fossey identified and made contact with nine gorilla groups, consisting of eighty gorillas. Each of these groups provided Fossey with unique and special experiences. But there were three groups that influenced Fossey the most during those early years: Groups 4, 5, and 8. It was from these groups that Fossey amassed the majority of her research about the behavior of mountain gorillas and the various aspects of their lives.

From the beginning Fossey named the gorillas in her study groups. She also often described them in terms of human charac-teristics and emotions, even though to do so was generally frowned upon by the scientific community. Describing animals in terms of human characteristics is called anthropomorphism. Most scientists at that time strongly cautioned against anthropo-morphism because they believed it pre-vented scientists from being objective and analytical in their research.

Yet even the eminent and highly re-garded scientist George Schaller was sur-prised and impressed by how much mountain gorillas resemble human beings in their physical appearance. He also ob-served and wrote about the many ways go-rillas act like human beings, even in things as simple as yawning in the morning when they awaken. Schaller was most impressed, however, with how much gorillas resem-bled human beings in their emotional ex-pressions. "They frown when annoyed," he wrote, "bite their lips when uncertain, and youngsters have temper tantrums when thwarted."[78]

Group 4

Fossey observed similar human character-istics in her study of Group 4. When Fos-sey first met Group 4, it consisted of four adult females, four younger females, one infant, and three males, one of whom she named Uncle Bert after one of her relatives. As Fossey humorously reported, "I considered the epithet a compliment, but my uncle never quite forgave me."[79]

Fossey named two of the females in the group Old Goat and Flossie. These two gorillas taught Fossey that there was sometimes a great deal of individual difference in the maternal instincts of female gorillas. One was very attentive and loving toward her offspring. The other was more aloof, or standoffish. "Flossie was very casual in the handling, grooming, and support of both of her infants," Fossey reported, "whereas Old Goat was an exemplary parent."[80]

In a television documentary called "Promises in the Mist," the narrator talks about the beautiful, penetrating eyes of a gorilla. "There are no words to explain how you feel when you look into the eyes of a gorilla," she says. "Something strikes a response in your soul. There's a kinship that makes you feel at ease."[81]

Pictures of some of the gorillas from Group 4. (Above) Flossie with the infant Cleo. (Left) Old Goat and son Tiger. Fossey was struck by the different parenting styles of Old Goat and Flossie.

Fossey must have felt the same way when she looked into the eyes of one female gorilla in Group 4 that she named Macho. *Macho* in Swahili means *"eyes."* It was Macho who provided Fossey with one of the most memorable experiences of her entire life at Karisoke.

The incident happened about ten years after Fossey first met Macho. Fossey had been out in the field observing Group 4, when finally Uncle Bert led the group away. Fossey made it a rule never to follow the gorillas once they left a certain spot because she did not want them to feel pursued and thus threatened. As she watched Group 4 disappear into the forest, she began to get ready to return to camp. Fossey relates in her book, *Gorillas in the Mist:*

> Suddenly, I heard a noise in the foliage by my side and looked directly into the beautifully trusting face of Macho, who stood gazing up at me. She had left her group to come to me. On perceiving the softness, tranquility, and trust conveyed by Macho's eyes, I was overwhelmed by the extraordinary depth of our rapport. The poignancy of her gift will never diminish.[82]

Digit

Group 4 eventually became one of Fossey's favorite groups to observe. This had to be, to a great extent, because of "a bright-eyed, inquisitive ball of fluff" that Fossey named Digit because he had a twisted or deformed finger.[83] From the beginning Digit seemed to be far more comfortable with humans than were many other gorillas. One reason for his ease

with humans, Fossey believed, was that there were no other gorillas in Group 4 who were close to Digit's age. Consequently, he had no one to play with. So, he was always happy to meet new humans and he always looked forward to his daily contacts with Fossey.

Through the years Fossey grew to care about Digit passionately. As she wrote, "I was unashamed to call him my beloved Digit."[84]

One day Fossey and wildlife photographer Bob Campbell were in the forest observing Group 4. On that day, Campbell captured on film a most remarkable and moving scene between Fossey and Digit. It showed Digit actually interacting with Fos-

Fossey's favorite gorilla, Digit, so named because of his twisted finger.

The Eyes of a Gorilla

Both Dian Fossey and George Schaller were captivated by the penetrating eyes of some of their subjects. As Schaller explains in The Year of the Gorilla:

"All their emotions are in their eyes, which are a soft, dark brown. The eyes have a language of their own, being subtle and silent mirrors of the mind, revealing constantly changing patterns of emotion that in no other visible way affect the expression of the animal. I could see hesitation and uneasiness, curiosity and boldness and annoyance. Sometimes, when I met a gorilla face to face, the expression in its eyes more than anything else told me his feelings and helped me decide my course of action."

The penetrating eyes of Fossey's beloved Digit, who she called "a bright-eyed inquisitive ball of fluff."

sey, something that had never before happened between gorillas and humans.

One of Fossey's biographers, Harold T.P. Hayes, describes that interaction in his book *The Dark Romance of Dian Fossey:*

In a sequence which seemed never to end, one experience more meaningful than the next, Digit became *involved* with Fossey. He didn't just touch her and then run away. First he took her glove in his hand and sniffed it, and then her pencil, and then he put that down and picked up her notebook and put it back down. Then, nestling in beside her, he rolled over and went to sleep.[85]

The film became part of a television documentary called "The Search for the Great Apes," which was shown throughout the world. Suddenly Digit and Fossey were famous. For most people the scene that was captured on film seemed to prove what Fossey had been saying all along. These were not ferocious creatures to be feared, but were actually gentle giants.

In the early 1970s the Rwanda Office of Tourism was attempting to attract more visitors to Rwanda. So an official at the office asked Fossey for a picture of a gorilla that they could use for a poster. She gave them a picture of Digit.

Soon thereafter, posters of the close-up shot of Digit began to appear in travel

In this picture, Digit's deformed finger is clearly visible. In the early 1970s, Digit's photo was used on posters to promote tourism in Rwanda.

offices around the world. Below the picture was a caption that read, "Come and See Me in Rwanda."

Although Fossey was as delighted as a proud parent to have Digit's picture appearing throughout the world, she was also concerned. She did not want tourists suddenly flocking to Karisoke and overcrowding the area. She was also afraid that tourists would bring viruses and diseases that would be harmful to the gorillas. Years later, her concerns would prove justified.

As Digit grew older, he had to assume more responsibility for the family unit and, as a result, had less time to play. Consequently, he gradually became less interested in humans.

One day in 1976 Fossey was in the forest observing Group 4 on a day that was cold and rainy. Digit, who by now served as sentry for the group, was about thirty feet from the other animals. For a moment Fossey thought about joining him, but then decided that she should respect his growing, teenage independence.

Instead, she settled down to watch the other Group 4 gorillas in the mist. But, then, something quite wonderful happened. "After a few minutes," she says, "I felt an arm around my shoulders. I looked up into Digit's warm, gentle brown eyes. He stood pensively gazing down at me before patting my head and plopping down by my side."[86] He was, indeed, her beloved Digit.

Group 5: A Strong Family Unit

Group 5 was also one of Fossey's favorite groups to observe during her first few years at Karisoke. When Fossey first met

Group 5, it consisted of fifteen members, including two silverbacks. Oddly enough, both of the silverbacks vocalized off-key, so Fossey humorously named the older silverback Beethoven and the younger silverback Brahms in honor of the famous composers. Later she identified a blackback in the group and named it Bartók to round out the musical trio.

One of the things that Fossey learned from this group was the easygoing and protective attitude male gorillas exhibited toward their young children. She also observed that male gorillas were very gentle with their offspring, despite the fact that a mature male might weigh as much as four hundred pounds. Beethoven was an excellent example of the extraordinary gentleness of the male gorilla. According to Fossey, he was "consistently indulgent and good-natured whenever his offspring tumbled in play around his huge, silvered bulk."[87]

One day, while observing the Group 5 gorillas sunning themselves, Fossey saw Beethoven gently pick up his youngest offspring, six-month-old Puck. He held the infant high above his head for a moment and then carefully groomed it before returning the baby to its mother. Throughout the years Fossey would observe such scenes often with other gorillas. Yet, it was that one encounter that for Fossey dispelled "all the King Kong mythology."[88]

When Fossey first came into contact with this group, all of the gorillas hid except one young fellow whom she named Icarus. Icarus loved to show off and, like many young human boys, could be mischievous one minute and appear totally angelic the next.

One day Icarus was swinging from a tree limb near Fossey when the limb broke, causing him to come crashing down. Beethoven and the other gorillas in the group came charging toward Fossey to see what all the noise was about. Just before they reached her, Icarus nonchalantly climbed back into the tree, acting totally innocent of causing the uproar.

Throughout the years Fossey watched this group closely as its makeup changed. She watched the youngsters grow and develop and mature and move out of the

Members of Group 5, Beethoven and Bartók, peer out of the brush.

group to start their own families. Years later, Fossey would remember this group fondly. "More than any of the five Karisoke study groups," she said, "the members of Group 5 have taught me how the strong bonds of kinship contribute toward the cohesiveness of a gorilla family unit over time."[89]

Group 8: An Affectionate Group

Throughout her years of field observation, Fossey witnessed numerous displays of affection among the gorillas. One of the most poignant happened one day between Rafiki, the aging silverback leader of Group 8, and Coco, an even older female mate. Together, the two reminded Fossey of two people who had been married for many years, both growing old together gracefully.

When Fossey first observed them that day, the two were more than 130 feet apart and out of sight of each other. Suddenly Rafiki seemed to call to Coco, who immediately started slowly climbing up the mountain in his direction. When Coco finally reached him, the two exchanged greetings, while Fossey watched intently at what happened next. As she remembers, "They looked directly into each other's face and embraced. She placed her arm over his back and he did likewise over hers. Both walked uphill in this fashion, murmuring together like contented conspirators."[90] It was, to Fossey, a remarkable display of affection.

Group 8 also included two youngsters, one of whom Fossey named Peanuts. One day, while Fossey was observing Group 8,

Icarus was an open show-off, often creating havoc within his family group to get attention. Fossey argued that such antics could only be explained by understanding that the gorillas had humanlike emotions.

Peanuts suddenly came up and sat down beside her. Fossey pretended to munch on vegetation to make the young male feel comfortable in her presence. She then slowly lay back in the foliage. At the same time, she extended her hand, palm up. "After looking intently at my hand," Fossey later recalled, "Peanuts stood up and extended his hand to touch his fingers against my own for a brief instant."[91]

The moment was over. But Peanuts, obviously as excited by this experience as Fossey, quickly beat his chest as he gave a youthful roar and then rushed off to rejoin his group. As for Fossey, the experience was so emotional and meaningful that all she could do was cry. It was the first time a human being had ever been touched by a gorilla.

Coco and Pucker

On March 4, 1969, a friend came rushing into Karisoke with distressing news. A young gorilla had been captured by poachers about six weeks earlier and was now confined in a small wire cage in the town of Ruhengeri at the base of Mount Visoke. Could Fossey come down the mountain, the friend wanted to know, to see if she could help the poor, defenseless animal?

Fossey rushed immediately to the park conservator's office. What she found when she arrived horrified her. A tiny, terrified infant gorilla was confined in a small box. It had been captured by one of the most notorious poachers in Rwanda for a zoo in Cologne, Germany. In the process of capturing the infant, more than ten adult gorillas trying to protect it were killed.

After being captured, the young female gorilla was tied with wire to a bamboo pole and carried down the mountain where it was put into a small wire cage. Eventually she was transferred to the conservator's of-

In a moment that Dian would remember for the rest of her life, the infant gorilla Peanuts touched her outstretched hand. (Above) Fossey with Peanuts before, and (right) after the moment.

A Close-Knit Family

Like both Schaller and Fossey, Walter Baumgartel recognized the humanlike qualities of the mountain gorilla. In this excerpt from his book Up Among the Mountain Gorillas, *Baumgartel tells about the day that he and his guide Reuben witnessed a gorilla family of three cross a path in front of them.*

"Apparently, the father did not like the look of things, for, as soon as he spied Reuben, he crossed . . . into the forest to our left. His mate followed him obediently. The youngster hesitated, however, and seemed curious to find out what was afoot. . . . When he realized he was left alone with such uncanny company, his courage failed and the frightened creature turned and ran back into the forest. Mother, now missing her child, returned just in time to see his little bottom disappear. She chased him, grabbed him by the hand, gave him a slap on the backside, and dragged him over the path into the forest, where father's impatient barking could be heard. This family scene, so touchingly human, changed my attitude toward gorillas. From that moment on, they were no longer mere animals to me; they were my relatives and there was no reason to be ashamed of the kinship."

fice in Ruhengeri, who was then going to send her to the Cologne zoo.

By the time Fossey saw the animal, the infant was near death, having spent twenty-six days in the tiny wire cage. "I shall never understand how the orphaned infant managed to survive the confines of the cage, her meager diet, or the infected wounds caused by the wire bindings," Fossey later said. "Somehow she had found the will to live."[92]

Fossey also learned that the conservator of the park was the one who had initially paid the poacher to capture a baby gorilla. To Fossey, that was an outrage. The conservator was the person whose job it was to protect the wildlife in the Parc des Volcans from poachers. The only reason he had sent for Fossey was that he was now afraid that the young infant might die. He wanted Fossey to take it back to camp and nurse it back to health.

Before Fossey left the village to return to Karisoke, she named the infant gorilla Coco, in honor of Group 8's Coco who had recently died. She then sent an important message to her camp staff. She wanted them to turn one of the rooms in her own two-room cabin into a miniature forest. "To ruin a room by bringing in trees, vines, and other foliage had seemed to them sheer nonsense," Fossey later said, "but they were used to my strange requests."[93]

As soon as Fossey got back to camp, she released Coco in her new habitat. Cautiously, the baby gorilla looked around. She then walked to a bench beneath the window. Fossey recalls:

With great difficulty, she climbed onto the bench and gazed out at the mountain. Suddenly she began to sob and shed actual tears, something I have never seen a gorilla do before or since. When it finally grew dark, she curled up in a nest of vegetation I had made for her and softly whimpered herself to sleep.[94]

For the first two days Coco's health seemed to be returning. Then she took a turn for the worse. Fossey was afraid she was going to die. On that day some men from the village arrived, carrying a box. In it was another young gorilla that Fossey learned had also been captured for the zoo but it, too, was badly injured.

Fossey named this gorilla Pucker. At first Pucker and Coco were not friendly but by the end of the day they were sleeping together in the special room Fossey had created originally for Coco.

For the next few weeks Fossey nursed the two young animals around the clock, abandoning her field studies so she could be with the two babies full-time. Twice during this time park guards came to get the babies. But Fossey convinced them that the gorillas were still too sick to travel.

Finally, the conservator himself came to the camp to demand that she release the gorillas. At first Fossey tried to convince the conservator that the animals

Dian with Coco and Pucker, the two gorillas that were entrusted to her care after they were found near death, captured by poachers. Unfortunately, Fossey could not keep the gorillas in safety and had to return them to be sold to zoos.

Coco and Pucker, who were destined to remain in zoos for the rest of their lives, died at the young age of ten years. Fossey remained heartbroken over their capture.

were still not well enough to travel. But he refused to listen. He threatened to send poachers to capture two other infants if Fossey did not release Coco and Pucker to him. Fossey realized that if the poachers tried to capture other infants, many more adults would be killed.

Reluctantly, she agreed to release them. And in May 1969, two months after they had first arrived in camp, porters carried Pucker and Coco down the mountain, never to return to their natural habitat.

Watching her two young friends being carried away was more than Fossey could bear. "I ran out of the cabin, ran through the meadows of our countless walks, and ran deep into the forest until I could run no more. There is no way to describe the pain of their loss."[95]

Coco and Pucker lived for another seven years at the Cologne zoo, then died in 1978 within a month of each other, each no more than ten years old. In the wild, mountain gorillas normally live to be fifty years old or more.

7 A Volatile Character

By 1969 Fossey decided that she wanted to conduct a thorough and exact gorilla census within the Virunga Mountains. It was a project that would eventually take more than eleven years.

Ten years earlier, George Schaller had estimated that there were between 400 and 500 mountain gorillas in the Virungas. Around Kabara alone, he found and studied 169 gorillas in ten different groups. By the time Fossey arrived at Kabara, she found only three groups totaling 52 animals.

Fossey knew that the census would be a long and difficult job, since she wanted to cover each of the six dormant Virunga volcanoes thoroughly. This meant exploring, as she put it, "every gully, ravine, and slope" in search of gorilla groups and then writing out detailed descriptions of the groups encountered.[96]

In order to undertake such a mammoth project as a census, Fossey reluctantly realized she would need help. There was simply no way she could conduct the census by herself, even though she disliked the idea of having other people at the camp.

For Fossey, the idea of conducting a census was exhilarating. There simply could be nothing better than, as she put it,

Dian, with her first census worker Michael Burkhart, unloads supplies from Lily. Fossey looked forward to providing an accurate census of the animals.

Karisoke camp would eventually attract students eager to work with Fossey. Once they arrived, however, they found Fossey aloof, demanding, and critical.

the challenge of the search, the thrill of encountering a new gorilla group, the awesome beauty of the mountains revealed by virtually every turn in a trail, and the pleasure of making a "home" with only a tent and the benevolence of nature.[97]

Clearly, not everyone saw the undertaking the same way. During the course of the next eleven years, more than twenty census workers came to Karisoke. Many, if not most, returned home after only a brief stay. Says Fossey somewhat humorously:

It never dawned on me that exhausting climbs along ribbons of muddy trail, bedding down in damp sleeping bags, awakening to don wet jeans and soggy boots, and filling up on stale crackers would not be everyone's idea of heaven.[98]

Many of the young students who came to Karisoke left simply because they couldn't withstand the rigors of living in a jungle or the physical exertion. One eager young man made the difficult three-hour climb to Karisoke only to collapse at Fos-

sey's feet gasping that he was simply not going to be able to take it. He returned to the United States immediately.

Many other students left because they couldn't adjust to life at a research camp in Africa. Fossey realized that in most field stations it was difficult for groups of strangers to live together harmoniously. But at Karisoke the difficulties were even more pronounced. The weather was often rainy and damp; the high altitude made it difficult to breathe; and the food was uninteresting. The worst part for most students, however, was the solitude. They simply couldn't take being alone in the field for days on end.

Even in camp there was very little socializing. When one doctoral student enthusiastically arrived at Karisoke, he expected stimulating, intellectual discussions about the gorillas. He expected to discuss his own research project in animal behavior. What he quickly discovered within days of his arrival was quite different:

Here ten thousand feet up on a volcano, were living three people, each cooking his own meal and then eating

Dian works by lamplight in her Karisoke cabin. Fossey preferred isolation to the company of people.

it in the silence of his own cabin. After the pressures of my exams I had been looking forward to some discussions about biological principles and research, particularly on gorillas. Yet here I was as isolated now as one is in an examination hall, surrounded by others yet unable to communicate with them. I began to think about my situation and I seemed to be sucked into a downward spiral of severe depression. Never before had I experienced such depression.[99]

Her Rigid Standards

Perhaps the biggest reason most students left, however, is that they simply couldn't get along with Fossey—or to be more exact, because sooner or later, she decided that they didn't measure up to her very high, very demanding, very rigid standards.

The Honesty of Gorillas

Fossey's affinity with gorillas and her difficulty with people and with personal relationships were explained in part by Ian Redmond, as quoted by Sy Montgomery in Walking with the Great Apes.

"Dian had been shat upon by a lot of people. Therefore she was very wary about entering into a relationship. She had been hurt.

But the gorillas were straight. They were honest in their feelings toward her. If they were angry, you could see they were angry; if they liked you, they showed it. It was very up front. Dian appreciated the honesty of the relationship you have with gorillas, and you don't owe them anything and they don't owe you anything, other than trust. With the gorillas she didn't have to hide her feelings from them. She had a very honest relationship with them."

Part of the problem was that the students who came to Karisoke usually expected one thing, and Fossey expected something quite different. The students were generally doctoral candidates, who were there to collect data for their theses. They also came to Karisoke expecting to work closely with the now-famous Dr. Fossey.

Yet Fossey expected the students to help maintain the camp, build new cabins and repair others, and help teach others how to track gorillas. But mostly, she insisted that they take part in anti-poaching patrols. She ordered them to track down poachers and bring them back to her as captives. In later years many people complained that Karisoke had ceased to be a research center and had instead become an armed camp. Eventually most students had to ask themselves which was more important: conducting research or chasing poachers.

To Fossey the answer was clear. To put their own needs ahead of the needs of the gorillas was simply unacceptable. In fact, it

was heresy. The gorillas had to come first. "As far as I am concerned," she said, "the gorillas are the reward and one should never ask for more than their trust and confidence after each working day."[100]

A Contradictory Character

Needless to say, there were many students who grew to despise Fossey. She could be both condescending and mean, calling her students *mtoto*, the Swahili word for children, or worse. It is easy to imagine Fossey telling her students that they had less sense than *soko-mutu mtoto* (baby chimps). According to most accounts, she mistreated everyone around her, including both her Rwandan staff and her graduate students. Even her best friend, Rosamond Carr, admitted that "working for her *was* impossible."[101]

To make matters worse, her temper was unpredictable. She could be talking calmly one minute and then fly into a rage

Dian speaks with students Sandy Harcourt (center) and Graeme Groom. Fossey was a critical taskmaster with the students, dismissing their complaints as whiney and immature.

An Abusive Temper

Over time Fossey became known for her unpredictable and abusive temper. In this excerpt from The Dark Romance of Dian Fossey, *Harold T.P. Hayes describes one incident that Kelly Stewart, a student, observed at Karisoke.*

"Stories circulated about how the madwoman on the mountain was abusing her African staff. Kelly Stewart had seen Fossey hit Rwelekana with a flashlight, and there were other incidents. Once, after a bitter argument, Fossey had refused to pay Rwelekana his wages. Finally, he decided to go along with her; he needed his pay. He thought that if he gave up and apologized she would reconsider. It wasn't quite so easy. Stewart says that Fossey made Rwelekana kneel before her and beg her forgiveness. Each time he offered his apologies, Dian—looming over him—would demand, 'What did you say, Rwelekana?' 'I said I'm sorry, Madame,' he repeated again and again. 'Say it louder. What did you say, Rwelekana?' 'It was just awful,' Stewart recalls."

the next. As one student recalls, "Dian could be impossible, but also a lot of fun. Trouble was, I never could be sure of which at any given moment."[102]

One day Fossey and one of her students were tracking gorillas when they came upon a meadow with hundreds of cows. Fossey insisted that they immediately abandon their search for gorillas and set out on a cattle roundup. She wanted to drive the cattle into the Zaire side of the border, where the park guards at that time were more strict.

Trying to herd hundreds of cows across the border, however, was not easy, since they would frequently wander off in different directions. Although her student was doing the best he could in herding the cows toward the border, Fossey didn't think he was doing a good enough job. Finally, she became totally exasperated with

him. "Dian shouted caustically that I wasn't much use 'sitting on my butt,' as she put it, and to 'make myself useful and bring them back.'"[103]

Fossey knew that she had a reputation for being difficult and demanding, even hot tempered. And at times she seemed to be bothered by the perception. She once told a student, "I'd love it if you could come and work with me at Karisoke. But you'd end up hating me."[104] When another student first arrived in camp, she told him, "I know you've heard a lot of bad stories about me, but the best thing to do is ignore them and concentrate on the gorillas."[105]

As time went on Fossey appeared to develop a split personality that even she seemed to recognize. One of her students remembers once seeing a painting that Fossey had painted of herself. "It was very schizophrenic," she says. "One half of the face was normal, the other was dark and brooding."[106]

Perhaps the worst, most shocking charge levied against her, however, came from Bill Weber, who worked with Fossey off and on for eight years. In the end, he says:

> She was riding on some kind of dedication she had once had. . . . She criticized others of "me-itis," yet she kept threatening to burn the [Karisoke research] station down and all the long-term records. She was willing to take down everything with her—Karisoke, the gorillas. When I did a census that indicated the gorilla population was growing quite nicely, she tried to cut off my funding; she wanted them to be dying.[107]

One student who did survive under Fossey's regime seemed to intrinsically understand her one unchangeable pronouncement about the gorillas better than anyone else. His name was Ian Redmond. Redmond stayed at Karisoke for two years. During that time he came to understand that Fossey basically did not trust people and that her abrasive nature was her way of testing them.

Redmond also felt that in some ways Fossey was like the gorillas she so dearly loved. As he once explained:

> If you are easily put off by bluff charges, screaming and shouting, then you probably think that the gorillas are monsters. But if you are prepared to sidestep the bluff charges and temper and shouting and get to know the person within . . . then you'll find that Dian, like the gorilla, was a gentle, loving person.[108]

And the fact is Fossey had a great sense of humor, wry and sardonic as it was. Once in the mid-1980s she captured a poacher whom she had captured once before ten years earlier. Looking at him, she commented dryly, "It bothers me that he doesn't look any older than he did then, but I look a millennium older, which isn't fair."[109]

On another occasion, at a time when she was nearly broke and unsure of where she was going to get enough money to keep Karisoke running, she lamented, "I

Fossey rests with her gorillas. Although Fossey could be irascible and temperamental, observers also claimed she had a wry sense of humor.

could try selling my body, but there wouldn't be many takers for Fossil Fossey."[110]

Nyiramachabelli

Fossey even found the nickname that the Rwandans gave her to be amusing, although many other people might have found it derogatory. She acquired the nickname one day when she was tracking Group 5 near the boundary between the park and the villagers' field. As she approached the area, which was on a bluff overlooking the farmland below, she heard the excited voices of the villagers screaming "Ngagi! Ngagi!" ("Gorilla! Gorilla!"), as they watched the gorillas sitting calmly on the bluff.

Moments later the gorillas wandered off at about the same time that Fossey climbed out on the bluff. Suddenly a new cry went up from the villagers. "Nyiramachabelli!" they yelled, as they saw this strange white woman standing on the bluff. "Nyiramachabelli."

Later, Fossey learned that Nyiramachabelli means "the old lady who lives in the forest without a man." "Although my new name was pleasantly lyrical," Fossey confessed humorously, "I would have to admit that I did not like its implications."[111]

Tragically, by the time she was murdered, Fossey had very few good friends left. Ian Redmond was one, of course, and Bob Campbell another. But for the most part, Fossey must have felt that she, too, like her gorillas, had been abandoned in the mist of the Virungas by most human beings. Fossey herself summed up her loneliness and sense of abandonment and

As Fossey grew older, she became more obsessed with saving the gorillas from poachers. Having lost many of her gorillas to them, she escalated her tactics and became hated by the natives.

isolation in her last letter to her friend Rosamond Carr, her closest friend in Rwanda. "Oh, Roz," she said sadly, "I need a friend so much. So many people are against me."[112]

There was, of course, her one true friend—Digit. In early December 1977, Fossey went into the forest to observe Group 4. She found Digit sitting alone away from the others. He was now a young silverback and his job was as a sentry, or lookout, for his family.

Finally, as Fossey got up to leave, Digit abandoned his post for just a moment. He picked up some foliage and walked over to Fossey. Then he smacked her on the back with it—his way of saying goodbye.

It would be the last time Fossey would see her beloved Digit alive.

8 The Death of a Friend

On January 2, 1978, the weather was beautiful in Karisoke. Fossey hadn't seen Group 4 for quite some time and she was concerned. So she and one of her trackers headed off in one direction and Ian Redmond and another tracker in the other, both looking for this special group.

Shortly before noon, Fossey was heading back to camp, having had no success in locating Uncle Bert's group, when suddenly, she saw Redmond running towards her. She froze as he looked sadly at her and then gave her the shocking news. "Digit has been murdered," he said almost solemnly.

A Devastating Loss

Thinking about that devastating moment years later, Fossey said:

> There are times when one cannot accept facts for fear of shattering one's being. As I listened to Ian's terrible words, all of Digit's life since my first meeting with him as a playful little ball of black fluff ten years earlier, passed through my mind. From that moment on, I came to live within an insulated part of myself.[113]

Fossey was devastated. "That tragedy practically unhinged her," says Mary Smith, of the National Geographic Society. "She became dangerous to herself and the Rwandans, because of her volcanic temper and her methods of interrogating alleged poachers."[114] Later Fossey told a friend that she wished she could have died in Digit's place.

Fossey sent her porters to bring Digit's body back to camp. There, only a few feet from her cabin, Digit was buried.

Soon afterwards Fossey learned that Digit had been killed on December 31, 1977, while trying to protect his family. Group 4 had been attacked by six poachers and their dogs. Digit, who was the rearguard defender, charged to cover the retreat of the rest of the group, which numbered thirteen. He was speared to death. The poachers then cut off his head and his hands and left his mutilated body to rot.

At the burial Fossey must have thought back over the years she had spent with this special friend. She undoubtedly recalled the many times she would visit Group 4 when Digit was a youngster. Fossey knew that Digit looked forward to those visits almost as much as she. Often during those visits he would coax Fossey into playing with him by "flopping over on to his back, waving stumpy legs in the air, and looking at me smilingly as if to say, 'How can you resist me?'"[115]

Publicizing Digit's Death

Fossey was determined not to let Digit die in vain. She and Redmond talked about what they might do. On one hand, they wanted to publicize Digit's murder because they knew the publicity would bring large sums of money into Rwanda for con-servation purposes. At the same time, she was afraid the money would not be used for what she wanted—to pay for more anti-poaching patrols. Nevertheless, they decided to launch a publicity campaign to bring international attention to Digit's death and the plight of the mountain go-rillas. They hoped that the publicity might help put pressure on the Rwandan gov-ernment to do something about the poachers.

Fossey immediately began a campaign to try to protect the gorillas. She wrote to the Rwandan government and to conser-vation groups to try to get pressure put on

Dian at Digit's grave. Digit's death by poaching seemed to push Fossey over the edge. Although it propelled her to begin several successful campaigns for conservation, the death also propelled her tactics to become more outrageous.

A Sad Farewell

The kinship of gorillas is poignantly expressed by Fossey in Gorillas in the Mist *when she describes the death of Kweli, Uncle Bert and Macho's only son.*

"On the morning of his death, he was found breathing shallowly in the night nest he shared with Tiger. Kweli had only enough strength to give faint screams and whines when the group slowly fed away from him. Responsive to Kweli's sounds of distress, the gorillas returned to his side repeatedly throughout the day to comfort him with belch vocalizations or gentle touches. . . . Every animal seemed to want to help but could do nothing. . . . [Finally] each member of the group went to Kweli individually to stare solemnly in his face for several seconds before silently moving off to feed. It was as though the gorillas knew Kweli's life was nearly over."

the government. She wanted poachers to receive a long prison sentence or even the death penalty. She also wanted the park guards to have the right to kill poachers within the park.

In addition, Fossey planned to have a new set of posters made featuring Digit. Only this time the poster would show Digit's corpse—without a head or hands. She would use the same slogan: "Come and See Me in Rwanda." "I know it sounds ghoulish," Fossey said, "but it might have some effect on the people who buy heads and hands."[116]

She also decided to launch the Digit Fund. The purpose of the fund, as Fossey envisioned it, was to support active conservation of gorillas. She wanted the money raised by the fund to be used specifically and exclusively to increase the number of guards patrolling the park area.

At that time Fossey explained her reason for establishing the fund:

To sit back and grieve and ignore the actual wanton human reason for his death is to do Digit a grave injustice. Perhaps, though, if the public has further knowledge of his life and personality, he can serve to protect those animals remaining.[117]

(Today, the Digit Fund is still in existence, although in 1992 its name was changed to the Dian Fossey Gorilla Fund to more accurately reflect the work that the group does.)

Soon after Digit's murder Fossey's men caught one poacher who Fossey believed was responsible for Digit's death. As Fossey gazed at the poacher standing before her, she was filled with rage. "I can't tell you," she later wrote to friends, "how difficult it was for me not to kill him."[118]

Eventually four of the six men who were responsible for Digit's death were captured. Fossey demanded that they be given life in prison. But each one was sen-

The effects of poachers are clearly seen in this dead silverback and the skeleton of another. Poachers kill the animals for their unusually large hands and feet, making souvenir items from them.

tenced to only three to five years in prison, and Fossey knew in her heart that they would be out in far less time. For Fossey, however, her sentence of sadness would be for life.

The Slaughter Continues

In a letter to the *National Geographic* about the murder, Fossey said, "I am now wondering if this is the beginning of the end . . . for if they get away with this killing, how much longer are the others going to last?"[119]

Unfortunately, the slaughter wasn't over. About seven months later, on July 24, one of Fossey's students found the body of Uncle Bert, the leader of Group 4. Soon after that, Fossey and her student found Uncle Bert's mate, Macho, the gorilla whose haunting eyes had so overwhelmed Fossey by the depth of the message they conveyed.

In the attack on the group, Uncle Bert and Macho's only offspring, Kweli, was badly wounded. He managed to live for another three months, however, before gangrene took his life.

Uncle Bert and Macho had been killed while they were asleep in their night nests. Most people suspected that the poachers had purposely selected this group to slaughter because they knew it was Fossey's favorite group.

Fossey, however, believed that the Rwandan park guards were responsible for the killings. "The publicity surrounding Digit's murder had generated foreign aid to help protect the remaining gorillas, and she believed that the guards wanted to make sure the money kept coming in."[120] Her theory, however, could never be proved.

Eventually a number of poachers was caught and accused of the murder. One, named Sebahutu, was sentenced to ten years in prison. He was released after only ten months.

The Mountain Gorilla Project

Soon after the murder of Digit, Sandy Harcourt, one of Fossey's students, came up with a different plan for protecting the mountain gorillas. This plan, which became known as the Mountain Gorilla Project, was designed to take into account the needs of the local people while protecting the gorillas at the same time. The way to do that was through the lucrative business of gorilla tourism.

The idea, which was backed by the Fauna and Flora Preservation Society and the African Wildlife Foundation, was to set up a three-part program for the conservation of the mountain gorilla: anti-poaching, education, and tourism.

The anti-poaching part of the program would continue the work that Fossey and the Rwandan government already had in place.

The education part of the program was designed to teach the local people about the importance of gorilla conservation. Even though the people of Rwanda had lived near the gorillas all of their lives, most Rwandans had never seen one. They did not understand the ecological importance of the gorillas to the rain forests.

Dian and Sandy Harcourt (left) had different ideas on how to save the gorillas. Harcourt wanted to promote tourism, which repelled Dian, who felt that the gorillas' way of life would be greatly disturbed.

Alan Goodall, a former student at Karisoke Research Centre who later became director, explains the ecological importance in a television documentary called "Promises in the Mist":

We get a lot of rain here and the forest soaks that rain up like a big sponge and then lets it out gradually. And if this area were cut down, not only would you lose the animals and these unique hagenias but the whole area would suffer rapidly from erosion.

"The gorillas are an important part of the tropical forest ecosystem," Goodall continues. "If the gorillas disappear and other species disappear, then the forest will disappear." There are many reasons for that, he says. For example, "seeds from some of the trees in the forest won't germinate unless they are in gorilla dung. It's

---

The Ecosystem of the Virungas

In The Wandering Gorillas, *Alan Goodall explains the ecological importance of the rain forests of the Virungas and the mountain gorillas and other animals.*

"If such large areas of forest continue to be cut down, the gorillas, and other animals such as elephant, buffalo, duiker, bushbuck and the few remaining leopards, will be forced higher and higher up the slopes of the volcanoes. If all the saddle areas between the peaks are eventually cultivated then the animal populations will stand, like so many islands, in an ever growing sea of cultivation. As the altitude increases so the vegetation of the area changes, not only in species composition but also in abundance; consequently the areas of suitable forage get smaller and smaller at higher altitudes. In addition some plant species have very long growth periods. A giant senecio, for example, may take up to two hundred years to reach its full size. A gorilla group which has been forced to spend more than its usual amount of time at these altitudes can destroy the tree in less than an hour while feeding on the under pith [core plant tissue]. At these altitudes rain and mist are much more frequent than lower down the mountain and the gorillas, who merely sit still during heavy rain, have less time to find their food. In addition, pneumonia, a major cause of death of the gorillas in this region, is bound to claim more victims at the higher, wetter altitudes. Infant mortality especially will inevitably increase."

In the 1970s, tourism seemed the only way to save the endangered mountain gorilla. If Rwanda could get tourists to spend money to see the gorilla in its natural habitat, they could raise money to prosecute poachers.

important for them to pass through the bodies of the animals," Goodall says.[121]

Tourism, however, was perhaps the most important part of the program. The plan was to make Rwanda an ideal place for tourists to see mountain gorillas. Tourists would bring money into the country—money for hotels and restaurants, guides and porters, souvenirs. It would also provide jobs for the people of Rwanda. If the gorillas were providing an income for the people, it would give the people an incentive to want to preserve the park and keep the mountain gorillas alive.

Fossey was adamantly against the plan. She found the idea of bringing tourists into the country to be totally distasteful. Those "idle rubberneckers," as she called them, would bring disease to the gorillas. As far as education of the people about conservation was concerned, she saw it only as a waste of time. As she wrote in a letter to Ian Redmond:

> *You*, of all people, know that cutting a trap is one hell of a lot more important than showing conservation education [films] to Africans. . . . The more popular the Mountain Gorilla Project grows, the less chance the gorillas have.[122]

9 Rumors, Myths, and Enemies

By the end of 1978 Fossey's campaign to publicize Digit's death and the plight of the mountain gorilla was succeeding. People from all over the world began donating money to the Digit Fund to help save the gorillas. They also bombarded the Rwandan government with critical letters demanding better protection for the gorillas.

The negative publicity that Fossey had created for Rwanda angered Rwandan government officials, and they, in turn, began complaining to the National Geographic Society and other groups which, for many years, had been funding Fossey's research at Karisoke.

At the same time, some people began spreading rumors about Fossey's mental health. The nicer rumors merely maintained that she was becoming "bushed." The more vicious ones claimed she had finally snapped and was clinically insane.

Sigourney Weaver, the actress who played Dian Fossey in the movie version of *Gorillas in the Mist*, strongly disagrees. "I don't think she really lost it," says Weaver, whose experiences in making the movie were so profound that she later became the honorary chairperson of the Digit Fund. "Her friends who loved her dearly sometimes thought she was acting crazy, but crazy with a small *c*," Weaver says. "She was desperate. The government wasn't supporting her. Her own scientific community wasn't supporting her. She didn't have anyone with whom she was sharing her life to balance her, no one to say, 'Well, Dian, here's another way of doing it.'"[123]

Actress Sigourney Weaver played Fossey in the movie Gorillas in the Mist. *Weaver, who studied Fossey to prepare for the role, believed the woman was desperate to save the gorilla, but not crazy.*

Dian is surrounded by guards who have confiscated slings used by poachers to ensnare animals. The presence of such guards brought criticism that Fossey had turned her research center into an armed camp.

A Persistent Controversy

The stories persisted. There were also stories about how she had turned the Karisoke Research Centre into an armed camp where she was torturing poachers. Finally, the rumors and the controversy surrounding Fossey became too much for the organizations that had been funding Karisoke. She had become an embarrassment to the scientific community and the various funding organizations decided she should leave Karisoke.

The governing board for the Karisoke Research Centre let it be known that they wanted her removed and replaced with a "more scientific" person. They wanted someone who would work to develop the gorilla sanctuary as an economic resource for Rwanda. Summing up the opinion of almost everyone on the board, one member said about Fossey at that time:

> She was a very sick woman. The life she had led and the terrible physical disabilities had worn her down. They had also seriously affected her judgment. All that she had built at Karisoke was in danger of falling down because of her fixation about poachers. The only hope was to get her out of it.[124]

In February 1979 Fossey received a cable from the National Geographic Society,

Fossey in the graveyard for the gorillas she had found killed by poachers.

one of the primary sources for her funding since she first established a research center at Kabara. "Received seriously disturbing reports concerning events [at] your camp," the message said. "Such encounters create concern and embarrassment [for] National Geographic."[125]

Even the American government entered the picture. The American ambassador received a letter from the U.S. secretary of state stating flatly that it was necessary for Fossey to leave the country for a while in order to calm relations with that country.

By now even her friends were encouraging her to take a break. They were concerned for her safety and her health, which had never been very good. They urged her to go to the United States to finish her book, which she had been working on for more than four years.

But Fossey resisted. If she left Karisoke, there would be no one to pro-

tect her gorillas, she said. Sarcastically, she added that without her to protect the gorillas, her book would have to be titled *And Then There Were None.*

By the end of 1979, in addition to her political difficulties Fossey was also having many health problems and was in pain almost constantly. Her hip hurt so badly that she was sure she had cancer. As a result, she was rarely able to venture into the forests to visit her gorillas.

At about the same time Fossey received an offer to teach at Cornell University in Ithaca, New York. So, finally, beaten down by political opposition and her own failing health, Fossey reluctantly accepted the teaching position to begin in March 1980.

During the summer of 1980 Fossey returned to Karisoke for a brief visit. She was heartbroken when she learned that Kima, her pet monkey, had died. Her dog Cindy was so sick that Fossey decided to take her back to the United States.

In September 1980 former student Sandy Harcourt was appointed to take charge of the Karisoke Research Centre. He had worked under Fossey earlier. Now that he was in charge of Karisoke, he wanted nothing to do with Fossey and he made it clear that she was not welcome at the camp. For the next three years Fossey was, in effect, barred from her adopted country.

A Sojourn in the United States

During those years Fossey continued to teach at Cornell, while also going on lecture tours around the country. In her speeches she would talk about the ongoing fight to save the endangered mountain gorillas. At the end of her talk, she would show a slide of the graveyard at Karisoke.

"I keep the graveyard as a memorial," she would tell people, "in the hopes that the day won't come when there are only graveyards and memories in the mist."[126]

By January 1982 Fossey began thinking about the possibility of returning to Karisoke. She knew, however, that she could never go back as long as Harcourt was there. But she had also heard that Harcourt was becoming unhappy with his position as director of the Karisoke Research Centre. He did not feel he was getting the proper support from the funding institutes or the money he needed to run Karisoke.

Then something unexpected happened. The board members of the Karisoke Research Centre suddenly began to feel that perhaps Fossey should become more directly involved with Karisoke once again. Anti-poaching patrols had virtually been abandoned since she was away, and a number of gorillas had been killed.

Fossey at Louisville Zoo in 1981. Fossey returned to the United States to accept a teaching position at Cornell University in New York.

Return to Karisoke

By early 1983 Fossey finally finished her book and began to make plans to return to Karisoke for a brief visit. In a letter to Ian Redmond she expressed her concern over what had happened to Karisoke during her absence:

> I *know* that poaching is heavier there, and within the Virungas as a whole, than ever when I was there. I *know* that young gorillas are being captured. . . . I also *know* the physical facilities at Karisoke are nearly rotted out because no one cared about the upkeep of the cabins; the car is finished for the same reasons. Everything I worked for nearly single-handedly over thirteen years is just about finished.[127]

Fossey arrived in Kigali on June 20, 1983. Because of her health problems, she was concerned about the high altitude and whether she would have problems breathing, but she climbed to camp. She had been away for three years and wondered whether or not the gorillas would remember her.

On July 5, 1983, she went into the lush green forests in search of Group 5. When she finally found the group, she began making noises like a gorilla. One of the first gorillas she saw was Tuck, whom she had known for almost fifteen years.

Fossey with the gorillas of Group 5 in 1979. When Fossey returned in 1983 the gorillas recognized Fossey, approaching her and surrounding her as if greeting a long-lost friend.

When Tuck saw her the gorilla did a double take. Then she walked up to Fossey. Fossey later recalled:

She stared intently into my eyes and it was eye to eye contact for thirty or forty seconds. Not knowing quite what to do, for I had never had this reaction from gorillas before, I squished myself flat on the bed of vegetation. Whereupon, she smelled my head and neck, then lay down beside me . . . and embraced me! . . . embraced me! . . . embraced me! GOD, she *did* remember![128]

Soon other gorillas from Group 5 joined Fossey and Tuck, each vocalizing in a warm and contented way. The gorillas spread out their arms and engulfed one another in a memorable, touching reunion. "I could have happily died right then and there," she later wrote, "and wished for nothing more on earth, simply because they had remembered."[129]

Fossey returned to the United States at the end of the summer to go on a book tour. It was not something she particularly looked forward to. "I reckon if people want to buy a book, they will buy it," she said. "They don't need the author shoving it down their throats."[130]

Nevertheless, she traveled throughout the United States and appeared on many different television talk shows. During this time she was awarded a medal of honor from the Humane Society of the United States. She also developed a new idea for the protection of mountain gorillas: the Guardians for Gorilla Groups.

Guardians for Gorillas

Fossey wanted each of the gorilla groups in the Virungas to have a special guardian group assigned to it. Each guardian group would consist of a small number of Rwandans, one of whom would make contact with their assigned gorilla group at least once every other day "so that the location and status of every gorilla within the Virungas would constantly be known to a central registry."[131] The guardian groups would also be paid and the program would be publicized to encourage foreigners to adopt a gorilla group and then contribute money for the support of that

Jane Goodall and Biruté Galdikas (far right) both received large grants to continue their work with primates while Fossey was struggling to make ends meet at Karisoke.

particular group's guardians. In return, these sponsors would receive regular communication about their guardian groups and how their gorilla groups were doing. "The idea is so simple," Fossey said, "it can hardly help but work."[132]

Although many people liked the idea, it never caught on fully. Many of the reasons for this were political. Since Fossey had gone ahead and set up a few guardian groups, she was now obligated to pay for them herself out of her already limited resources. She was even more discouraged about her finances when she learned that her two colleagues studying primates, Jane

Goodall in the study of chimpanzees and Biruté Galdikas in the study of orangutans, both had recently received sizable grants to continue their work. Then for Christmas that year (1983), Fossey received a donation to the Digit Fund of $10,000. It was the best Christmas present she had received in years.

Since Fossey's return to Rwanda in 1983, the Rwandan officials would issue a visa to her for only three months at a time. At the end of each three-month period, she would have to come down the mountain, drive for two hours by jeep to Ruhengeri and from Ruhengeri to Kigali, where she would wait, sometimes for days, to get her visa renewed. It was a long, difficult, almost tortuous trip for Fossey, particularly since she now suffered greatly from emphysema, made worse by years of heavy smoking.

Ups and Downs

Despite this annoyance, Fossey felt that 1984 had gone very well for the gorillas. Her anti-poaching patrols had been extremely successful. During the year, the anti-poaching staff had cut down more than two thousand traps, released eighteen animals alive, and caught seven poachers who were imprisoned. Most importantly, during that year, none of the Fossey gorillas had been captured or killed by poachers.

By early 1985 Fossey was worried about whether her visa would be renewed. Her enemies were once again saying that she should be prevented from staying in Rwanda because she had "abused the country's laws and hospitality."[133] So she was surprised and enormously relieved, as she explained in a letter to a friend, when she learned that her visa was renewed for six months:

> I don't believe I could have borne it if they had told me to leave [Rwanda]. The longer I work here, despite the fact that I cannot go into the field as often as I used to, I realize more and more just how important it is that I am here. . . . This is the only place where I belong.[134]

In April of that year she signed a contract with Universal Studios for $150,000 for a movie to be made based on her book. At last she would have the financial resources to keep her anti-poaching patrols working and to maintain her camp.

That summer Nunkie, one of her gorillas, was found dead. An autopsy showed that he had died from hookworm, a human parasite. The news distressed Fossey a great deal because she knew it was possible for the gorillas to get the parasite simply by being in close contact with humans, by touching them. Since she was responsible for the habituation of the gorillas in the first place, she feared that she herself might be responsible for causing their death. She was devastated.

After the death of Nunkie, Fossey warned her students not to breathe on a gorilla, and certainly not to visit the gorilla groups if they were feeling sick. She was afraid that a virus could cause an epidemic among the gorillas that could wipe them out entirely.

By fall of 1985 Fossey was hearing reports that there was a movement under way to take the camp away from her once again. The people who were formulating this plan had convinced the Rwandan government that Fossey was costing the government a great deal of money since she kept the tourists away from the study groups. They wanted to take over her camp and turn it into a tourist camp, run by the Mountain Gorilla Project. Fossey was adamant in her determination not to let anyone have her camp. As she put it, "they'll have it over my dead body, if then."[135]

In August she once again had her visa renewed, but this time for only two months. That same month Wayne McGuire, an American doctoral student from Oklahoma University, arrived at Karisoke to begin his research work. Little

Competition with Jane Goodall

From the beginning Fossey was jealous of Jane Goodall and the attention Goodall received. In Fossey's mind, she was always living in Goodall's shadow, as Sy Montgomery expresses in her book Walking with the Great Apes.

"Neither Dian nor her gorillas seemed able to compete successfully with Jane and her chimps for the limelight. Dian made important discoveries about gorilla life: how females transfer, either voluntarily or via raids from rival silverbacks, out of their natal [birth] groups; how a raiding silverback will sometimes kill the infants of a mother he is kidnapping to bring her into heat so he can mate with her; how gorillas will sometimes eat their own dung to recycle nutrients. But these discoveries were outshone by Jane's findings about chimpanzee hunting and tool use, cannibalism and warfare—behavioral aspects that made the chimps seem more like man."

Jane Goodall speaks about chimpanzees and other primates. Goodall's likable personality enhanced her ability to continue to receive grants for her work.

Wayne McGuire arrived at Karisoke in 1985.

did McGuire know at that time that his presence at Karisoke would eventually change his life forever.

After McGuire arrived he was shown to his cabin, where, exhausted, he fell asleep until the next morning. Suddenly, at 8:30 A.M., he heard a loud voice yelling, "Hey, McGuire, are you going to spend your next two years inside that cabin?"[136] It was McGuire's introduction to Dian Fossey.

From the beginning, her treatment of McGuire was vintage Fossey—cool, aloof, sarcastic, even nasty. About him, she once said, "He's a nice boy but with hardly the smarts to come in out of the rain."[137] Another time she told a friend that she was planning to fix this new young student dinner at her cabin, which was only a short walk from his cabin, but was worried about whether or not he would be able to find his way there.

In October Fossey's visa was renewed for yet another two months. One night later that month, she could not sleep. So she stepped outside of her cabin to get some air. At her doorstep she found what biographer Farley Mowat has described as "the wooden image of a puff adder [snake]."[138] Over the years Fossey had learned about *sumu*, or black magic. So she knew that the puff adder meant that someone had put a curse on her—the curse of death.

Once again, on December 3, it was time to make the long trip down the mountain to renew her visa. This time she was totally shocked but thrilled when she learned that it was going to be renewed for two years:

> She went running around Kigali, hugging everyone she saw and telling them, "Now I can go up on the mountain in absolute peace. I don't have to go down again. I've got a visa for 2 years." She was literally over the moon.[139]

Three weeks later, Dian Fossey would be dead.

10 A Tragic End

The headline on page 15 of the *New York Times* read: "Zoologist Is Slain in Central Africa." The story went on to report that Fossey, an American zoologist, had been slain by unknown assailants in the early morning hours of Thursday, December 27.

Almost immediately people began to speculate about who might have killed Fossey. Some said it had to be one or more of the poachers she had fought against so vigorously during her eighteen years in Africa. Others thought it might have been someone on her camp staff, someone whom she had mistreated so terribly over the years. Still others thought that the park conservator or the Rwandan government itself might have had something to do with it.

What everyone did agree on, however, was that there simply was no end to the list of people who may have wanted to see Dian Fossey dead.

Four days later, on a gray and gloomy afternoon on the last day of 1985, Dian Fossey's body was placed in an unpainted plywood coffin, which was then put into the ground next to her beloved Digit in the gorilla graveyard. Fossey herself had placed a simple numbered marker on the grave of each of the gorillas she had buried there—Uncle Bert, Macho, and her beloved Digit, among them. Her marker was number 16.

Fossey's coffin is lowered into the ground. Fossey's death was the subject of much controversy as people tried to figure out how and why Fossey had been killed. Most believed that it was vengeful poachers who grew tired of Fossey's aggressive tactics to end their trade.

Few people who knew Fossey were surprised by her murder. In fact, if there was any surprise at all, it was that Fossey had managed to survive as long as she did. Kelly Stewart, a former student who today has few kind words for Fossey, said unemotionally, "It was a perfect ending. She got what she wanted. It was exactly how she would have ended the script."[140]

Arrests and Accusations

"Dian kufa! Dian kufa!" Those words still bring chills to McGuire as he thinks back to that tragic morning. When he arrived at Fossey's cabin, which was a short walk from his own, he discovered that it had been totally ransacked, with drawers pulled open and things thrown everywhere. Yet, oddly enough, many valuable items were not touched, including $1,200 in cash.

The killer or killers had gotten in by ripping away a sheet of tin that formed the wall of her bedroom. Why Fossey did not immediately hear the intruder no one knows for sure. Perhaps she had taken a sleeping pill, or perhaps her food had been drugged earlier in the evening.

A few days after the murder five Rwandans were arrested. Eight months later four of them were released. The fifth, a tracker who had worked for Fossey for more than ten years, reportedly hanged himself in jail on August 22.

That same month the Rwandan authorities charged American graduate student Wayne McGuire with the murder of Dian Fossey. They said he killed her out of professional and personal jealousy.

McGuire, who had been trying to run the Karisoke Research Centre since Fossey's murder, was shocked, and not just a little bit scared. He maintained that he and Fossey had had an excellent relation-

Student Wayne McGuire was charged with Fossey's death. Many feel Rwandan authorities charged McGuire in an effort to hide the true killers.

A Fatal Personality

In his book African
Madness, *author
Alex Shoumatoff
quotes Bill Weber
about one of the
motives for Fossey's
murder.*

"Dian could have had all the accolades [praise] in the
world for what she did during the first six years. It would
have been natural for others to build on her work, but
she didn't have the self-confidence or the character for
that to happen. So many people came over here inspired
by Dian Fossey, prepared to give her the benefit of the
doubt. No one wanted to fight her. No one wanted to
take over the place. She invented so many plots and enemies. She kept talking about how nobody could take it
up there, how they all got "bushy", but in the end she
was the only one who went bonkers. She didn't get killed
because she was saving the gorillas. She got killed because she was behaving like Dian Fossey."

ship. "We had no serious professional
problems and we were good friends," he
said.[141]

His friends and attorney told him that
he should try to flee the country. But
McGuire did not want to do that. First of
all, he maintained that he was innocent
and, second, that he had to finish his research work. If he left the country now, he
would have to start all over on a new thesis
for his doctorate.

Finally, McGuire realized how serious
the situation was and, not wanting to face
a Rwandan court, he escaped to the
United States. Even though the Rwandan
authorities knew he was at the airport in
Kigali, they did not try to stop him. Perhaps they even wanted him to escape. In
any event, he was tried for the murder of
Dian Fossey in absentia in December 1986
and was convicted. He was then sentenced
to death by firing squad.

To this day McGuire maintains that he
had nothing to do with Fossey's murder.
"Dian's death was a terrible tragedy, not
only because of the cruelty of the act but
also because it shortened her struggle to
save her beloved gorillas," McGuire says,
adding ruefully, "I don't think we'll ever
know for sure who killed her, because
we'll never get the facts out of the Rwandans. . . . I feel sorry for Dian, and sorry
for the gorillas. They may be the ultimate
victims of this sad story."[142]

McGuire also says he thinks he knows
why the Rwandan authorities accused him
of the murder: "If Dian Fossey was killed
by a poacher in the park, that might not
be good for tourism," he says. "So blame it
on an American and see to it he's pres-
sured to get out of the country."[143]

Most people agree that McGuire is
telling the truth, that he did not kill Dian
Fossey. But if he did not kill her, who did?

Who Killed Dian Fossey?

Alex Shoumatoff, author of *African Madness*, says that Fossey's death may have been the result of a simple burglary gone awry:

> In 1981, while she was at Cornell, a burglar broke into her cabin [at Karisoke] in precisely the same way—by snipping out the tin sheet below her bedroom window—and made off with a camera. The burglar could have tried again five years later. This time Dian was there. The burglar grabbed the nearest weapon—her panga—and killed her, and fled in panic without taking anything.[144]

Farley Mowat, author of *Woman in the Mists*, has a different point of view. He believes she was killed by someone she knew, an African, perhaps, who was familiar with the camp and its day-to-day activities. "I suspect he was hired . . . by influential people who increasingly viewed Dian as a dangerous impediment to the exploitation of the Parc National des Volcans, and especially to the exploitation of the gorillas."[145]

Sy Montgomery, author of *Walking with the Great Apes*, has a more philosophical view of who killed Dian Fossey:

McGuire (right) views Fossey's grave. Mystery continues to surround Fossey's death. The true killers will probably never be found.

Fossey's grave bears a testament to her love of the gorilla. Natives believe that her soul still resides in the area, among her beloved gorillas.

By imposing her own laws on a sovereign nation, by making enemies of local people instead of friends, by caring more about gorillas than people, Dian was just as reponsibile for her death as the person who wielded the panga that split her skull.[146]

Fossey's friend Ian Redmond has, perhaps, the most logical theory about why she was killed. In a letter that Fossey wrote to him about a month before she was murdered, she told about a recent incident in which park guards captured a poacher and brought the poacher to her. In searching him, Fossey found his *sumu*, or magic charms, which she confiscated, before he was taken away to jail.

Redmond believes that even though the poacher was in jail, he hired one or more friends or relatives to break into Fossey's cabin to get his *sumu* back. Redmond says:

> This man had something he felt was of vital importance as protection to himself, and Dian took it. I think it explains the illogical nature of the crime, that they searched the house and didn't steal anything valuable to a European.[147]

It is possible, then, that the assassin(s) did not actually intend to kill Fossey. She may have awakened and in a sudden struggle to escape was bludgeoned to death with a machete.

The Importance of Dian Fossey

Three years after Fossey's death a tombstone was placed at her grave. It reads:

Her Many Enemies

In his book The Dark Romance of Dian Fossey, *Harold T. P. Hayes explains why there were many people who might have wanted to see Fossey dead.*

"In pursuit of her singular goal, the protection of the endangered mountain gorilla, Fossey had shot at her enemies, kidnapped their children, whipped them about the genitals, smeared them with ape dung, killed their cattle, burned their property, and even sent them to jail. Anyone who dared to threaten her gorillas, or even to challenge her methods, set her off, and the force of her malevolence was difficult to imagine."

Nyiramachabelli
Dian Fossey
1932-1985
No one loved gorillas more;
Rest in peace, dear friend;
Eternally protected;
In this sacred ground;
For you are home;
Where you Belong.

In her book *Gorillas in the Mist,* Fossey notes that there is a tradition in Rwanda that says "the souls of the good will spend their eternity on the summit of Karisimbi."[148] Today, there are those who believe that it is on this summit—the summit of the 14,782-foot Mount Karisimbi—that the soul of Dian Fossey can be found.

A Lasting Legacy

In October 1990, five years after Dian Fossey's brutal murder, a civil war broke out in Rwanda between a rebel group called the Rwanda Patriotic Front and the Rwandan government. For three years the war raged throughout the tiny country, forcing more than a million Rwandans to flee and putting an end to Rwandan tourism.

Because of the threat of violence during this time, the staff members of the Karisoke Research Centre were also forced

A soldier confronts two natives during the Rwandan civil war in 1990. The war caused the Karisoke Research Centre to be abandoned.

to abandon the center. It was the first time that the center was closed since Fossey founded it more than twenty-five years earlier. As a result, the center was vandalized and most of the supplies, such as radios and computers, clothing, and cooking utensils, were stolen.

Finally, in August 1993, the Rwandan government signed a peace treaty with the Rwanda Patriotic Front, and the staff of the Karisoke Research Centre began the difficult task of repairing and restocking it.

Unfortunately, peace didn't last long. In April 1994 Rwanda's president was killed in a suspicious plane crash. Soon afterward, fighting broke out again and tens of thousands of people were massacred.

During this time, the biggest threat to the gorillas came from the hundreds of thousands of Rwandans who were forced to flee from their homes into neighboring Zaire. As one anthropologist explained, "The greatest amount of disturbance has been the pushing through the forest of people and their pushing of cattle ahead of them."[149]

In August 1994, however, researchers and some anti-poaching workers returned to Karisoke. Although the center had been trashed and looted, the researchers were able to confirm that nearly all of the research gorillas at the Karisoke Research

Fossey with gorillas. Fossey's work continues in the efforts of people who attempt to rescue the mountain gorilla from extinction.

Centre had survived the fighting and the mass exodus through the Virunga mountains by people on their way to Zaire.

Yet, the situation in Rwanda remained extremely dangerous and by the end of the summer, park wardens and anti-poaching patrols were forced to flee once again, not knowing when they might be able to return. Without them, there continues to exist a real danger for the future of the mountain gorillas as a result of the fighting, the fleeing refugees, and poachers.

Mountain Gorillas' Future Remains Uncertain

Today, it is estimated that there are 650 mountain gorillas in Rwanda, Zaire, and Uganda, up from the 242 that Fossey found during her first gorilla census in 1981. This increase is, in itself, a tribute to the work Dian Fossey began more than twenty-five years ago.

Yet, the long-term survival of the mountain gorilla is still in jeopardy. As researchers point out, "Prospects for the survival of the gorillas will be considerably improved if their conservation takes into account the needs of human populations in the region along with those of gorillas and the Virunga Volcano ecosystem."[150]

The Dian Fossey Gorilla Fund (DFGF), which operates, directs, and finances the Karisoke Research Centre, says that the Rwandan government understands the importance of the gorillas as both a scientific and economic resource for the poor country. "We believe the Rwandans appreciate the value of these rare animals to their country, no matter who has the governmental power," a DFGF spokesperson said.[151]

Consequently, the DFGF remains dedicated to working with the Rwanda government in the conservation of the mountain gorilla. In the past it has employed Rwandans for daily anti-poaching patrols and to track the gorilla groups' movements for research purposes. It has supported an international education program, helping both the people of Rwanda and throughout the world to understand the importance of the mountain gorillas.

Most importantly, perhaps, the DFGF has provided an opportunity for research scientists and students to study mountain gorilla behavior, thereby helping to ensure a future for the "uniquely noble" animals to whom Dian Fossey dedicated her life.

Notes

Introduction: A Life Devoted to the Gentle Giants

1. Wayne McGuire, "I Didn't Kill Dian. She Was My Friend," *Discover*, February 1987.
2. Jane Goodall, "Mountain Warrior," *Omni*, May 1986.
3. George B. Schaller, *Gorilla: Struggle for Survival in the Virungas*. New York: Aperture Foundation, 1989.
4. Schaller, *Gorilla*.
5. Dian Fossey, "More Years with Mountain Gorillas," *National Geographic*, October 1971.
6. Charles Krupp, "Sigourney Weaver Defends Dian Fossey," *Glamour*, October 1988.
7. Gilbert M. Grosvenor, president of the National Geographic Society, quoted in Letters to the Editor, *National Geographic*, May 1986.
8. Quoted in Alex Shoumatoff, *African Madness*. New York: Knopf, 1988.

Chapter 1: A Lonely Beginning

9. Sy Montgomery, *Walking with the Great Apes*. Boston: Houghton Mifflin, 1991.
10. Quoted in Harold T.P. Hayes, *The Dark Romance of Dian Fossey*. New York: Simon & Schuster, 1990.
11. Quoted in Farley Mowat, *Woman in the Mists*. New York: Warner Books, 1987.
12. Quoted in Mowat, *Woman in the Mists*.
13. Quoted in Hayes, *The Dark Romance*.
14. Quoted in Mowat, *Woman in the Mists*.
15. Quoted in Shoumatoff, *African Madness*.
16. Quoted in Mowat, *Woman in the Mists*.
17. Dian Fossey, *Gorillas in the Mist*. Boston: Houghton Mifflin, 1983.
18. Fossey, *Gorillas in the Mist*.
19. Fossey, *Gorillas in the Mist*.

Chapter 2: Africa: The Land of Her Dreams

20. Fossey, *Gorillas in the Mist*.
21. Fossey, *Gorillas in the Mist*.
22. Quoted in Hayes, *The Dark Romance*.
23. Hayes, *The Dark Romance*.
24. Fossey, *Gorillas in the Mist*.
25. Fossey, *Gorillas in the Mist*.
26. Walter Baumgartel, *Up Among the Mountain Gorillas*. New York: Hawthorn Books, 1976.
27. Quoted in Mowat, *Woman in the Mists*.
28. Alan Goodall, *The Wandering Gorillas*. London: William Collins Sons, 1979.
29. Hayes, *The Dark Romance*.
30. Fossey, *Gorillas in the Mist*.
31. Quoted in Mowat, *Woman in the Mists*.
32. Quoted in Mowat, *Woman in the Mists*.
33. Quoted in Virginia Morell, "Called 'Trimates,' Three Bold Women Shaped Their Field," *Science*, April 1993.
34. Quoted in Mowat, *Woman in the Mists*.
35. Quoted in Mowat, *Woman in the Mists*.
36. Fossey, *Gorillas in the Mist*.

Chapter 3: From Kentucky to the Congo

37. Fossey, *Gorillas in the Mist*.
38. Baumgartel, *Up Among the Mountain Gorillas*.
39. Fossey, *Gorillas in the Mist*.
40. Quoted in Fossey, *Gorillas in the Mist*.
41. Fossey, *Gorillas in the Mist*.
42. Fossey, *Gorillas in the Mist*.
43. Fossey, *Gorillas in the Mist*.
44. Fossey, *Gorillas in the Mist*.
45. Dian Fossey, "The Imperiled Mountain Gorilla," *National Geographic*, April 1981.
46. Dian Fossey, "Making Friends with Moun-

tain Gorillas," *National Geographic*, January 1970.

47. Fossey, *Gorillas in the Mist.*

48. Fossey, *Gorillas in the Mist.*

49. Fossey, *Gorillas in the Mist.*

Chapter 4: A New Beginning

50. Rosamond Carr, "Lonely Struggle of the Gorilla Lady," *International Wildlife*, December 1988.

51. Fossey, *Gorillas in the Mist.*

52. Mowat, *Woman in the Mists.*

53. Quoted in Hayes, *The Dark Romance.*

54. Quoted in Hayes, *The Dark Romance.*

55. Quoted in Virginia Morell, "Dian Fossey: Field Science and Death in Africa," *Science 86*, April 1986.

56. McGuire, "I Didn't Kill Dian."

57. Montgomery, *Walking with the Great Apes.*

58. Fossey, *Gorillas in the Mist.*

59. Montgomery Brower, obituary in *People*, February 17, 1986.

60. Fossey, *Gorillas in the Mist.*

61. Quoted in Shoumatoff, *African Madness.*

62. Hayes, *The Dark Romance.*

63. Quoted in Montgomery, *Walking with the Great Apes.*

64. Quoted in Mowat, *Woman in the Mists.*

65. Quoted in Montgomery, *Walking with the Great Apes.*

Chapter 5: Poachers and Cattle Herders

66. Quoted in Mowat, *Woman in the Mists.*

67. Hayes, *The Dark Romance.*

68. Fossey, *Gorillas in the Mist.*

69. Montgomery, *Walking with the Great Apes.*

70. Morell, "Called 'Trimates.'"

71. Montgomery, *Walking with the Great Apes.*

72. Quoted in Morell, "Called 'Trimates.'"

73. Quoted in Brower, *People.*

74. Fossey, *Gorillas in the Mist.*

75. Fossey, *Gorillas in the Mist.*

76. Fossey, *Gorillas in the Mist.*

77. Quoted in Hayes, *The Dark Romance.*

Chapter 6: The Study Groups at Karisoke

78. George B. Schaller, *The Year of the Gorilla.* Chicago: University of Chicago Press, 1964.

79. Fossey, *Gorillas in the Mist.*

80. Fossey, *Gorillas in the Mist.*

81. KUSA-TV, "Promises in the Mist," a documentary produced by KUSA-TV, Denver, CO.

82. Fossey, *Gorillas in the Mist.*

83. Fossey, *Gorillas in the Mist.*

84. Fossey, "More Years with Mountain Gorillas."

85. Hayes, *The Dark Romance.*

86. Fossey, *Gorillas in the Mist.*

87. Fossey, *Gorillas in the Mist.*

88. Fossey, *Gorillas in the Mist.*

89. Fossey, *Gorillas in the Mist.*

90. Fossey, *Gorillas in the Mist.*

91. Fossey, *Gorillas in the Mist.*

92. Fossey, *Gorillas in the Mist.*

93. Fossey, "Making Friends with Mountain Gorillas."

94. Fossey, *Gorillas in the Mist.*

95. Fossey, *Gorillas in the Mist.*

Chapter 7: A Volatile Character

96. Fossey, *Gorillas in the Mist.*

97. Fossey, *Gorillas in the Mist.*

98. Fossey, *Gorillas in the Mist.*

99. Goodall, *The Wandering Gorillas.*

100. Quoted in Montgomery, *Walking with the Great Apes.*

101. Quoted in Hayes, *The Dark Romance.*

102. Quoted in *Digit News*, Dian Fossey Gorilla Fund, Englewood, CO, May 1993.

103. Goodall, *The Wandering Gorillas.*

104. Quoted in Montgomery, *Walking with the Great Apes.*

105. Quoted in McGuire, "I Didn't Kill Dian."

106. Hayes, *The Dark Romance.*

107. Quoted in Shoumatoff, *African Madness.*

108. Quoted in Shoumatoff, *African Madness.*

109. Quoted in Mowat, *Woman in the Mists.*

110. Quoted in Mowat, *Woman in the Mists.*

111. Fossey, *Gorillas in the Mist.*

112. Quoted in Shoumatoff, *African Madness.*

Chapter 8: The Death of a Friend

113. Fossey, *Gorillas in the Mist.*

114. Quoted in Morell, "Called 'Trimates.' "

115. Fossey, *Gorillas in the Mist.*

116. Quoted in Mowat, *Woman in the Mists.*

117. Dian Fossey, quoted in *Digit News*, Dian Fossey Gorilla Fund, Englewood, CO, May 1993.

118. Quoted in Montgomery, *Walking with the Great Apes.*

119. Quoted in Mowat, *Woman in the Mists.*

120. Hayes, *The Dark Romance.*

121. Alan Goodall, quoted in "Promises in the Mist," a documentary produced by KUSA-TV, Denver, CO.

122. Quoted in Mowat, *Woman in the Mists.*

Chapter 9: Rumors, Myths, and Enemies

123. Quoted in Krupp, "Sigourney Weaver Defends Dian Fossey."

124. Quoted in Mowat, *Woman in the Mists.*

125. Quoted in Montgomery, *Walking with the Great Apes.*

126. Quoted in Mowat, *Woman in the Mists.*

127. Mowat, *Woman in the Mists.*

128. Mowat, *Woman in the Mists.*

129. Fossey, *Gorillas in the Mist.*

130. Quoted in Mowat, *Woman in the Mists.*

131. Quoted in Mowat, *Woman in the Mists.*

132. Quoted in Mowat, *Woman in the Mists.*

133. Mowat, *Woman in the Mists.*

134. Quoted in Mowat, *Woman in the Mists.*

135. Quoted in Mowat, *Woman in the Mists.*

136. McGuire, "I Didn't Kill Dian."

137. Quoted in Mowat, *Woman in the Mists.*

138. Mowat, *Woman in the Mists.*

139. Montgomery, *Walking with the Great Apes.*

Chapter 10: A Tragic End

140. Quoted in Shoumatoff, *African Madness.*

141. McGuire, "I Didn't Kill Dian."

142. McGuire, "I Didn't Kill Dian."

143. McGuire, "I Didn't Kill Dian."

144. Shoumatoff, *African Madness.*

145. Mowat, *Woman in the Mists.*

146. Montgomery, *Walking with the Great Apes.*

147. Quoted in Brower, *People.*

148. Fossey, *Gorillas in the Mist.*

Epilogue: A Lasting Legacy

149. "Rare Mountain Gorillas are Mostly Unharmed After Wars in Rwanda," *New York Times*, August 30, 1994.

150. Quoted from a press release from the Dian Fossey Gorilla Fund, September 3, 1993.

151. Public relations letter dated September 3, 1993, from the Dian Fossey Gorilla Fund.

For Further Reading

Allan Carpenter and Matthew Maginnis, *Rwanda.* Chicago: Childrens Press, 1973. A description of the people, wildlife, geography, and culture of this poor country in East-Central Africa.

Jane Goodall, *Jane Goodall: My Life with the Chimpanzees.* New York: Pocket Books, 1988. Exciting autobiography by one of the pioneers of primate study in Africa.

————, *Jane Goodall's Animal World.* Macmillan Children's Group, 1990. One in a series of books about the wildlife of Africa, this one written by the famous primatologist herself.

Leah Jerome, *Dian Fossey.* New York: Bantam, 1991. An easy-to-read biography that includes photographs, maps, and line drawings of Fossey and her gorillas.

Bettyann Kevles, *Watching the Wild Apes: The Primate Studies of Goodall, Fossey, and Galdikas.* New York: Dutton, 1976. A good introduction to the work of Louis Leakey's "trimates": Jane Goodall, who worked with chimpanzees, Fossey, who worked with mountain gorillas, and Biruté Galdikas, who studied orangutans.

Anne Malatesta and Ronald Friedland, *The White Kikuyu: Louis S.B. Leakey.* New York: McGraw-Hill, 1978. Biography of the famous anthropologist who sponsored Fossey's early work, including his fascinating early childhood in East Africa, and his startling discoveries into the past of humans.

Kay McDearmon, *Gorillas.* New York: Dodd, Mead, 1979. Easy-to-read text with photos provides up-to-date research on the study of primates in Central Africa.

Susan Meyers, *The Truth About Gorillas.* New York: Dutton, 1980. An informative study of wild gorillas that reveals the gentle, peace-loving nature of these animals.

Mina White Mulvey, *Digging Up Adam: The Story of L.S.B. Leakey.* New York: David McKay & Co., 1969. A good biography of the anthropologist and his adventurous career.

Works Consulted

Walter Baumgartel, *Up Among the Mountain Gorillas*. New York: Hawthorn Books, 1976. Interesting personal adventure by the man whose hotel in the village of Kisoro was the required meeting place in the 1960s and early 1970s for all gorilla seekers.

Dian Fossey, *Gorillas in the Mist*. Boston: Houghton Mifflin, 1983. Fossey's own detailed account of her life and work at Karisoke includes both scientific reporting and details of her personal struggle to protect the mountain gorillas.

———, "The Imperiled Mountain Gorilla," *National Geographic*, April 1981.

———, "Making Friends with Mountain Gorillas," *National Geographic*, January 1970. The first of only three magazine articles Fossey wrote for *National Geographic* magazine about her study of the mountain gorillas.

———, "More Years with Mountain Gorillas," *National Geographic*, October 1971.

Alan Goodall, *The Wandering Gorillas*. London: William Collins Sons, 1979. A balanced account of life at Karisoke Research Centre during the 1970s by a former graduate student at the camp, who later became the director of the center.

Harold T.P. Hayes, *The Dark Romance of Dian Fossey*. New York: Simon & Schuster, 1990. A good biography with an extensive bibliography.

Wayne McGuire, "I Didn't Kill Dian. She Was My Friend," *Discover*, February 1987. Important article by the man convicted by Rwandan authorities of Fossey's murder.

Sy Montgomery, *Walking with the Great Apes*. Boston: Houghton Mifflin, 1991. Easy-to-read account of Fossey and Leakey's other two "trimates"—Jane Goodall and Biruté Galdikas.

Farley Mowat, *Woman in the Mists*. New York: Warner Books, 1987. A definitive biography with extensive quotations from Fossey's private letters and diaries.

George B. Schaller, *Gorilla: Struggle for Survival in the Virungas*. New York: Aperture Foundation, 1989. Beautiful, full-color photography of Rwanda and the Virunga Mountains adds to this informative look at both the people and the animals.

———, *The Year of the Gorilla*. Chicago: University of Chicago Press, 1964. Required reading for serious students of primatology.

Alex Shoumatoff, *African Madness*. New York: Knopf, 1988. A short but interesting account of Fossey's life focusing on the difficulties she encountered during her later years in Africa.

Index

on relating to gorillas, 40

U.S. Department of State, 41

Veschuren, Jacques, 25
Virunga Mountains
  census of gorillas in, 70-71, 101
  discovery of mountain gorillas in, 13
  first gorilla studies in, 14-15
  Fossey invited to, 31
  living in the, 36, 47-49, 51, 71-72
  location of, 13
vocalizations, 38-39

Walking with the Great Apes (Montgomery)

on dangers to gorillas from human contact, 89
on dealing with poachers, 56
on Fossey's death, 97-98
on the honesty of gorillas, 72
Watts, David, 51
Watusi, 12, 40, 43
  rights to herding in the Virungas, 54
  see also Tutsi
Weaver, Sigourney, 84
Weber, Bill, 75
wild celery, 38
witchcraft, 56, 93
Woman in the Mists (Mowat)
  on Fossey and poachers, 46
  on Fossey's home in

Louisville, 23
on Fossey's murder, 97

Year of the Gorilla, The (Schaller), 39-40
  on the eyes of a gorilla, 62
  on a first encounter with the mountain gorilla, 30
  on human fascination with gorillas, 12

Zaire, 13, 41
  gorilla protection in, 59, 74
  Rwandan refugees and, 100
Zimbabwe, 22
zoos, 53, 66, 69

Credits

Grateful acknowledgment is made to reprint excerpts from *Gorillas in the Mist* by Dian Fossey. Copyright © 1983 by Dian Fossey. Reprinted by permission of Houghton Mifflin Company. All rights reserved.

About the Author

For more than twenty-five years, Jack Roberts has worked as an editor and writer of educational materials for elementary and junior high school students and teachers, first at Children's Television Workshop and then at Scholastic Inc.

In addition, he has written several books for young readers, including a junior high school textbook on computer literacy as well as biographies of President Bill Clinton, South African civil rights leader Nelson Mandela, and U.S. Supreme Court Justice Ruth Bader Ginsburg.

Roberts lives in Princeton, N.J., and hopes one day to visit the gorillas of the Virungas.